# WINDOWS

### AND

# MIRRORS

## EXPLORING THE PARABLES OF JESUS

## JOHN C. BOWLING

The Foundry Publishing
PO Box 419527
Kansas City, MO 64141
thefoundrypublishing.com

978-0-8341-3890-2

Printed in the United States of America

Cover Design: Donnie Johnson
Layout: Michael J. Williams

Library of Congress Cataloging-in-Publication Data

Names: Bowling, John C., 1949- author.
Title: Windows and mirrors : exploring the parables of Jesus / John C. Bowling.
Description: Kansas City, MO : The Foundry Publishing, 2020. | Includes bibliographical references. | Summary: "Windows and Mirrors dives into some of Jesus's best-loved parables (and some less familiar ones) in order to explore the rich symbolism, deep emotion, and eternal perspective these stories have to offer. The author demonstrates how these tales are both mirrors in which we see ourselves reflected, and windows through which we can see into the heart of God"-- Provided by publisher.
Identifiers: LCCN 2019041047 (print) | LCCN 2019041048 (ebook) | ISBN 9780834138902 (paperback) | ISBN 9780834138919 (ebook)
Subjects: LCSH: Jesus Christ--Parables.
Classification: LCC BT375.3 .B69 2020 (print) | LCC BT375.3 (ebook) | DDC 226.8/06--dc23
LC record available at https://lccn.loc.gov/2019041047
LC ebook record available at https://lccn.loc.gov/2019041048

The internet addresses, email addresses, and phone numbers in this book are accurate at the time of publication. They are provided as a resource. The Foundry Publishing does not endorse them or vouch for their content or permanence.

All the proceeds from the sale of this book will go to the general scholarship fund of Olivet Nazarene University.

10 9 8 7 6 5 4 3 2 1

"Even in an age when men know less and less of the Bible, and care less for it, it remains true that the stories Jesus told are the best known stories in the world."[1]

—William Barclay

1. William Barclay, *And Jesus Said: A Handbook on the Parables of Jesus* (Philadelphia: Westminster Press, 1970), 9.

To Doris Cheeseman
*More than a mother-in-law*

# Contents

# Introduction

I will open my mouth with a parable; I will utter hidden things, things from of old.

—Psalm 78:2

Regardless of age, background, culture, language, or personality, everyone loves a story. When someone starts to tell a story at dinner, in a class, around a campfire, or at a family gathering, everyone will begin to lean in and listen intently. A well-told story makes a speech worth remembering, a class worth taking, an event worth attending, and a book worth reading. Stories are like the windows in a house: through a window, we can glimpse the wider world, gain a wider perspective, and see beyond ourselves.

Stories have been around since the dawn of creation. In his book *Story: The Power of Narrative for Christian Leaders*, Dr. Jay Martinson writes, "From cradle to grave, stories infuse meaning into our lives. They entertain, teach, inspire, comfort and confront."[1] He then notes, "Narratives have the power to do far more than merely entertain and teach. They can inspire us to change our lives. Stories are not merely things we read, hear, or watch. Stories are things we live. We understand and express our lives narratively . . . Our stories define who we are."[2]

1. Jay Martinson, *Story: The Power of Narrative for Christian Leaders* (Kansas City: Beacon Hill Press, 2016), 9.
2. Martinson, 10.

My mother-in-law has lived in a lovely retirement center for the past fifteen years. She is now in her early nineties, and recently, she decided to change apartments. Her long-time apartment was very convenient and cozy, and she had lived there long enough that it had become home, not just a place to live. Nonetheless, she decided to move. She was not moving to another town, another retirement center, or another wing of her present facility. Rather, she decided to move to the apartment right next door—just a few feet away from where she had lived for years. My wife and I wondered: why go through the stress and disruption of such a move? Did she just want a change? The new apartment was a little larger, but did she really need more room?

The desire for change and a little more space may have been factors. However, after visiting my mother-in-law's new place, it was clear that the primary difference between her previous apartment and her new one was that the new apartment had twice as many windows, including a huge picture window that overlooked a lovely small lake with a fountain. She hadn't been able to see the water from her old apartment, even though she'd been just as close—the windows made the difference. The windows expanded her world and enriched her view.

Windows help us see beyond ourselves and beyond our past experiences. The parables of Jesus are the same way—they provide new perspectives and new vistas to our understanding of life. They are windows that help us see the kingdom of heaven. Each story is a window into God's heart, revealing his grace and goodness.

The parables are also like mirrors. They provide ways for us to see ourselves. American playwright Arthur Miller once observed, "In every successful drama there is something which makes a person say, 'Hey! That's me!'"[3] In such a moment, the story or the play suddenly becomes a mirror in which we see ourselves, and that self-recognition yields some measure of self-understanding.

Shauna Niequist writes, "A story is never about one person. It has a full cast of characters, connected by blood or love or jealousy. There's nothing small or inconsequential about our stories. There is, in fact, nothing bigger. And when we tell the truth about our lives—the broken parts, the secret parts, the beautiful parts—then the gospel comes to life, an actual story about redemption, instead of abstraction and

---

3. Arthur Miller quoted in Shaun Lewis, "The Tale of Two Sons," Civil Servant Ministries, accessed September 1, 2019, https://www.civilmin.org/luke-15-11-32/.

theory."[4] In the same way, Jesus' parables are more than stories about other people; each reveals some aspect of ourselves.

Human beings are story-shaped. We live on a thin thread that stitches together what was, to what is, and, ultimately, to what will be. Steve Garber picks up this idea, saying, "In our imaginings, in our longings, at our best and at our worst, we are people whose identities are formed by a narrative that begins at the beginning and ends at the ending—the story of Scripture itself, of creation, fall, redemption and consummation—and from beginning to end we are torn by the tensions of our humanity, glorious ruins that we are."[5]

Jesus knew the value of telling stories; this is why he communicated so many of his teachings in the form of parables. Mark 4:34 says, "He [Jesus] did not say anything to them without using a parable. But when he was alone with his own disciples, he explained everything." Similarly, Matthew 13:1–3a says, "That same day Jesus went out of the house and sat by the lake. Such large crowds gathered around him that he got into a boat and sat in it, while all the people stood on the shore. Then he told them many things in parables . . ."

In Matthew 13:10–16, Jesus further explains his use of parables:

The disciples came to him and asked, "Why do you speak to the people in parables?"

He replied, "Because the knowledge of the secrets of the kingdom of heaven has been given to you, but not to them. Whoever has will be given more, and they will have an abundance. Whoever does not have, even what they have will be taken from them. This is why I speak to them in parables:

"Though seeing, they do not see;
    though hearing, they do not hear or understand.
In them is fulfilled the prophecy of Isaiah:
"'You will be ever hearing but never understanding;
    you will be ever seeing but never perceiving.
For this people's heart has become calloused;
    they hardly hear with their ears,
    and they have closed their eyes.
Otherwise they might see with their eyes,
    hear with their ears,

---

4. Shauna Niequist, *Bittersweet: Thoughts on Change, Grace, and Learning the Hard Way* (Grand Rapids: Zondervan, 2010), 240.

5. Steve Garber, *Visions of Vocation: Common Grace for the Common Good* (Downers Grove, IL: InterVarsity Press, 2014), 202.

understand with their hearts
and turn, and I would heal them.'

But blessed are your eyes because they see, and your ears because they hear."

Later, in Matthew 13:34–35, we read, "Jesus spoke all these things to the crowd in parables; he did not say anything to them without using a parable. So was fulfilled what was spoken through the prophet: 'I will open my mouth in parables, I will utter things hidden since the creation of the world.'"

These references underscore the importance of parables in Scripture. They are among the most-read and best-loved parts of the Bible, and so have become familiar and pervasive—even nonbelievers speak of "burying one's talents," being "a good Samaritan" or "counting the cost" without realizing that they are referencing Jesus's teachings. The parables have become part of the lexicon of everyday conversation, even among those who do not understand their significance.

These stories are filled with strong characters, vivid images, and rich symbolism, all delivered in tales from everyday life. Some of the parables are as brief as a single sentence, such as this word picture: "The kingdom of heaven is like yeast that a woman took and mixed into about sixty pounds of flour until it worked all through the dough" (Matthew 13:33b). Others, such as the story of the prodigal son, unfold in a sequence of scenes over many verses. All were simple and memorable enough to survive in an oral tradition before being transcribed after Christ's death.

But these stories are more than instructive; they are designed to foster recognition and stir emotion. And most importantly, they demand a response. These simple stories ask a question: how does our faith in Christ make a visible difference in our lives? Thus, the parables of Jesus are also invitations to believe and belong to a new kingdom—the kingdom of God.

Some parts of the Bible offer soaring rhetoric (for example, "They will soar on wings like eagles" in Isaiah 40:31), while others provide words of comfort ("The LORD is my shepherd" in Psalm 23). Some sections focus on history or theology. The parables are different in that they paint pictures; they are simple stories that illustrate profound truths.

Our word "parable" is derived from a Greek term, *parabolē*, that literally means "to place side by side for the sake of comparison." A parable, then, is a simple story that compares earthly matters to spiritual truths.

*Nelson's New Illustrated Bible Dictionary* defines a parable as "a short, simple story designed to communicate a spiritual truth, religious principle, or moral lesson; a figure of speech in which truth is illustrated by a comparison or example drawn from everyday experiences."[6] Another way to think of it is as "an earthly story with a heavenly meaning."[7]

Jesus's stories did not make use of mythology or fantasy. They aren't like Aesop's fables or Greek mythology, in which personified creatures or natural elements teach moral lessons. Rather, his parables grew out of true-to-life illustrations. Parables were Jesus's way of helping people with the transition we each must make every day—from our natural, earthbound life to new life in the kingdom.

Figures of speech add color and texture to our everyday communication. But in doing so, they do more than adorn language; they convey abstract ideas. From the start of his teaching ministry, Jesus used a variety of metaphors, similes, and analogies in the form of parables.

## Metaphor

A *metaphor* is a figure of speech in which a word or phrase literally denoting one object or idea is used in place of another to suggest a likeness between them. In other words, a metaphor compares seemingly unrelated subjects.

Throughout his ministry, Jesus made metaphors out of objects and ideas that everyone listening would have been familiar with: salt, light, bread, shepherds, vines, doors, and so on. The meaning of these metaphors was fairly clear and straightforward.

## Simile

A *simile* is a comparison that uses "like" or "as." For example, "as strong as a horse" or "as quick as a shot" are simple, straightforward similes that need little explanation. For an example of Jesus's use of simile, see Matthew 10:16, in which Jesus instructs his disciples to be "as shrewd as snakes and as innocent as doves."

6. *Nelson's New Illustrated Bible Dictionary* (Nashville: Thomas Nelson, Inc., 1995), 943.

7. William Barclay, *And Jesus Said: A Handbook of the Parables* (Philadelphia: Westminster Press, 1970), 12.

## Analogy

An *analogy* is a figure of speech that implies that if two things agree with each other in some respects, they will probably agree in others. An analogy is often used to make a difficult idea easier to understand. For example, we might say that life is like a journey, and then we go on to compare the situations that might occur over the course of a life to stops or encounters that someone might have on a long journey.

## Allegory

Though it is similar to other rhetorical comparisons, an *allegory* is generally longer and more detailed than a metaphor. While an analogy appeals to reason or logic, an allegory appeals to the imagination. Allegories can be long and complex. *Pilgrim's Progress*, by John Bunyan, *The Divine Comedy*, by Dante Alighieri, and *Animal Farm*, by George Orwell, are all books with allegorical characters and plots.

As he further developed his public ministry, Jesus moved beyond metaphors, similes, and analogies to the use of parables. The Bible records more than forty of these stories.[8] Some, such as the parable of the good Samaritan and the parable of the prodigal son, are well known, while others, such as the parable of the weeds, are more obscure. One thing all the parables have in common is that they provide a window into the kingdom, and a mirror in which we see our lives in light of that kingdom.

## Why Parables?

There are several historical and relational explanations for why Jesus may have favored parables as a primary teaching method.

**They were a common teaching method during Jesus's time.** Many of the great rabbis and other teachers of Jesus's day employed stories in their lessons. For example, the Old Testament tells the story of the prophet Nathan confronting King David with his sins involving Bathsheba and Uriah:

> The LORD sent Nathan to David. When he came to him, he said, "There were two men in a certain town, one rich and the other poor. The rich man had a very large number of sheep and cattle, but the poor man had

---

8. See "Appendix: The Parables of Jesus" for a full list of Jesus's parables found in the New Testament.

nothing except one little ewe lamb he had bought. He raised it, and it grew up with him and his children. It shared his food, drank from his cup and even slept in his arms. It was like a daughter to him.

"Now a traveler came to the rich man, but the rich man refrained from taking one of his own sheep or cattle to prepare a meal for the traveler who had come to him. Instead, he took the ewe lamb that belonged to the poor man and prepared it for the one who had come to him."

David burned with anger against the man and said to Nathan, "As surely as the LORD lives, the man who did this must die! He must pay for that lamb four times over, because he did such a thing and had no pity."

The Nathan said to David, "You are the man! This is what the LORD, the God of Israel, says: 'I anointed you king over Israel, and I delivered you from the hand of Saul. I gave your master's house to you, and your master's wives into your arms. I gave you all Israel and Judah. And if all this had been too little, I would have given you even more. Why did you despise the word of the LORD by doing what is evil in his eyes? You struck down Uriah the Hittite with the sword and took his wife to be your own. You killed him with the sword of the Ammonites. Now, therefore, the sword will never depart from your house, because you despised me and took the wife of Uriah the Hittite to be your own.'"

(2 Samuel 12:1–10)

- **Parables make difficult principles easier to understand.** The more abstract an idea, the harder it is to communicate. Jesus's parables featured characters and events that listeners recognized from their everyday lives and to which they could easily relate.
- **Parables allow people to discover truth for themselves.** By using parables, Jesus empowered listeners to contemplate new concepts and connect the dots between them. Discovered truth has a way of sticking with us in a more meaningful way.
- **Parables are memorable.** Jesus wanted people to hear and remember his teaching, discuss and ponder their meaning, then share what they learned with their families, friends and neighbors. Because Jesus's parables were simple and memorable, listeners could easily repeat them to others.
- **Parables allowed Jesus to teach controversial ideas covertly.** The religious leaders of Jesus' day were always looking for something to use against him, and parables made it difficult for these leaders to accuse him of heresy—he could hardly be arrested for telling stories. Parables allowed Jesus to speak words of rebuke or warning, but in a veiled manner.

## Principles of Interpretation

R. T. Kendall, who served for many years as the pastor of Westminster Chapel in London, writes that there are three principles we should keep in mind when considering the parables:[9]

1. **Not all parables are alike.** The parables address a variety of subjects, including the nature of the kingdom, the nature of the gospel, and the end times. Still others touch on stewardship and spiritual growth.
2. **Most parables have one central truth.** This means that when we read or listen to the parables, we should seek to discern the overarching message Jesus was communicating.
3. **Not every aspect of a parable is symbolic or didactic.** We need to be careful not to distort the parables' meaning by reading ideas or symbolism into them that Jesus never intended. We should note that context is key and can often unlock a parable's meaning. What prompted the parable? Who was Jesus's audience?

It is also important to remember that the parables were heard rather than read. An audience needed to be able to grasp the main point of the story without re-reading or studying the material. This is why the parables always started with the familiar—so that listeners could better grasp the new and unfamiliar.

The following chapters are designed to refresh our understanding of the parables and encourage us to apply the truths these stories contain—to see in each story a window and a mirror. As the master said, "Whoever has ears to hear, let them hear" (Mark 4:9).

9. R. T. Kendall, *The Parables of Jesus: A Guide to Understanding and Applying the Stories Jesus Told* (Grand Rapids: Chosen Books, 2004), 19–20.

# 1

# The Parable of the Soils

Matthew 13:3-9, 18-23

The Story

A farmer went out to sow his seed. As he was scattering the seed, some fell along the path, and the birds came and ate it up. Some fell on rocky places, where it did not have much soil. It sprang up quickly, because the soil was shallow. But when the sun came up, the plants were scorched, and they withered because they had no root. Other seed fell among thorns, which grew up and choked the plants. Still other seed fell on good soil, where it produced a crop—a hundred, sixty or thirty times what was sown. Whoever has ears, let them hear.

—Matthew 13:3–9

Listen then to what the parable of the sower means: When anyone hears the message about the kingdom and does not understand it, the evil one comes and snatches away what was sown in their heart. This is the seed sown along the path. The seed falling on rocky ground refers to someone who hears the word and at once receives it with joy. But since they have no root, they last only a short time. When trouble or persecution comes because of the word, they quickly fall away. The seed falling among the thorns refers to someone who hears the word, but the worries of this life and the deceitfulness of wealth choke the word, making it unfruitful. But the seed falling on good

17

soil refers to someone who hears the word and understands it. This is the one who produces a crop, yielding a hundred, sixty or thirty times what was sown.

—Matthew 13:18–23

## The Window

Matthew records this as the first of Jesus's parables. In some ways, this story is the most important parable because it illustrates the nature of parables and how to interpret them. In addition, this is one of the few parables found in all three of the synoptic gospels (see Mark 4:1–20 and Luke 8:1–15). The parable is followed immediately by Jesus's own interpretation and discussion of its meaning.

For the Galilean audience who first heard it, this parable would have evoked a very familiar scene. They had all seen a farmer walk his field with a bag slung across his shoulders, scattering seed. The seeds would be gently plowed into the soil before the early rains that caused the seeds to germinate. Then the farmer would watch and wait throughout the growing season for the later rains that brought the crop to its final fruition.

This is one of the few parables that Jesus explained to his disciples. There are four elements in this story: the sower, the seed, the soil, and the harvest. Each element is important, but the third element—the soil—is most important.

### The Sower

The parable begins with a character: "A *farmer* went out to sow his seed" (13:3, emphasis added). Those words provide a portrait of God, the Father, the sower and mover who takes initiative. Moreover, God is extravagant in sowing the seed everywhere.

What is described in the parable is true in our lives as well. God continues to be an extravagant God, giving us life, breath, health, opportunity, and most importantly, the seeds of the kingdom of God.

### The Seed

The second element of the parable is the seed. We don't have to wonder what the seed represents—when Jesus's disciples ask for the meaning of the parable, he says, "The farmer sows the word" (Mark

4:14). The seed represents the gospel, the message of God. Thus, this parable begins with God, the sower, sowing the seeds of the gospel.

## The Soils

Next comes the third and primary element of the story—the four different soils upon which the seed falls. These represent four different conditions of the human heart in responding to God's Word.

### The Pathway

The pathway is the soil that has been hardened by constant wear. This represents a hard heart in which it is difficult for the Word of God to take root. Jesus says that when the Word of God is sown in this soil, the birds of the air come and carry it away before it has a chance to grow.

This part of the parable illustrates how some who hear the gospel already have their defenses up—they are resistant to spiritual things. There is an inherent warning here: we must not let our lives become hardened to the things of God.

### The Rocky Ground

The second type of soil is rocky ground—a terrain that's common in Israel. In many places, the bedrock is so close to the surface that plants cannot develop a strong root system. As Jesus explains to his disciples, these are the people who hear God's Word and receive it joyfully. But shallow ground represents a shallow heart. These "shallow" Christians are enthusiastic at first, but once opposition, difficulties, or temptations come, they have no spiritual root system to anchor them, and they fall away.

### The Thorny Ground

The seeds sown among the thorns seem to have a better chance for growth and development than the seeds that fall on the pathway or on shallow ground. Here, the seed takes root and begins to grow—and would continue to do so, except for the thorns that compete with the seed for water and nutrients. Eventually, the thorns spring up and choke out the shoot. What is illustrated here is a kind of double life. This heart tries to have it both ways—it attempts to cultivate the good seed while also harboring the thorns. These are "both/and" people—people who want to follow God, but aren't willing to give up the world's pleasures and priorities to do so.

Have you ever noticed that weeds do not need any encouragement? Flowers and vegetables require nurturing, but weeds just pop up every-where. The same is true in our lives—we have to nurture what is good, but sin grows with little or no prompting.

Jesus identifies four types of weeds or thorns that will choke the seed of God's Word: 1) the cares of this world, 2) the deceitfulness of riches, 3) the desires for other things, and 4) the pleasures of life. There is nothing inherently wrong with any of these things, but if they come between us and our pursuit of God's kingdom and righteousness, our spiritual lives will suffer.

The pathway is hard; the rocky ground is shallow; the thorny ground is crowded. However, the good news is that there is also good ground with rich, receptive soil.

### The Good Soil

Here the seed finds a place to take root and grow. If we're willing to listen for the voice of God, even if we are skeptical; if we will meditate on what we hear; if we don't let our lives become cluttered with the things of the world; if we are open and receptive—the seeds can take root. And when that happens, blessings follow.

### The Harvest

Taken as a whole, the primary meaning of the parable is this: good seed requires good soil in order to bear good fruit. God can do amazing things in our lives if we receive his word—he longs to bless and fill our lives with joy and significance.

### The Mirror

Several years ago, not long after the construction of Benner Library and Resource Center at Olivet Nazarene University, the university decided to use a generous gift from the Gerald Decker family to trans-form what had been a rather barren space between the library and the student center into "the Decker quad."

The quad was designed as a large "O" with the names of senior class presidents and student council presidents around the brick walkway.

*John* ⟩

The sidewalks were expanded, and at the south end, a small stage was erected for campus gatherings. Shrubs were planted to beautify the area, and benches were placed throughout it.

All these features were important parts of the plan, but the heart of the entire project was placed in the center of a large raised area bordered with brick and stone. There, with great pageantry, the university planted the Tree of Learning.

It was then that the story turned humorous—and not so humorous at the same time. Within a few weeks of the dedication of the quad and the planting, the tree's leaves began to wither, then fall. The revered Tree of Learning, which was to be the university's living symbol of the pursuit of knowledge, died!

Very quickly, the dead tree was uprooted and replaced with a healthy new sapling. But little by little, the new tree also began to wane. Of course, jokes soon followed: "Did you hear that the tree of learning keeps dying?"

Eventually, the university, with the help of a good horticulturist, diagnosed the problem: there wasn't sufficient soil for a tree's roots to grow below the newly paved and bricked quad. The tree simply could not flourish without strong roots.

With renewed vigor and enhanced understanding, the university planted a new tree in better soil. Sure enough, once the root system began to spread, the tree flourished, and the symbol of learning was once again alive and well. The tree in the quad is a metaphor for life: we all must have a strong and healthy root system if we are to thrive.

When I left home to attend college, I was accompanied by two friends, Rick and Bruce, who had graduated high school with me just a few months before. While we were students, I had the opportunity to see this parable unfold in my friends' lives.

Rick and Bruce were very much alike. They grew up in the same town, attended the same church, and went to the same school. They had essentially the same socioeconomic background; in fact, they were first cousins, and even shared the same last name. So when we arrived at college, they had equal opportunities to be successful.

In the months that followed, I watched as Bruce chose to focus his time and energy on pursuits that would help him succeed as a student. I also watched as Rick (who was also my roommate) allowed others to make those important choices for him. As Bruce began to take hold of his life, Rick began to drift.

At first, Rick seemed to do well. As a freshman, he was a member of the inter-collegiate baseball team. He loved sports and he would talk to me from time to time about his desire to be a teacher and coach. However, he never got around to taking the necessary steps to make his dream come true. I watched as he began to self-destruct and neglect his studies. As a result, the following year, his poor grades kept him from playing baseball.

Rick's primary purpose for being at school—to play baseball—was gone. His hopes for the future began to fade. When we went home at the end of our second year, Rick went home for good—never to finish college, never to teach or coach, never to be what he could have been.

At the same time Rick was going home, Bruce was maximizing his university experience. He had to work hard, but his grades were good. He became active in campus activities. He set his sights on a career in business and took steps that would help him excel. As a result, Bruce began to reap the benefits of a college education. He graduated on time, got a good job, and later became an executive in a great company.

Rick and Bruce were in the same environment with the same opportunities. For one, the seed took root and bore fruit. For the other, the prospects of earning a university degree seemed good at first—but other things soon crowded out that possibility.

## Conclusion

An aspect of this parable that is often overlooked is the reference to a harvest of "a hundred, sixty or thirty times what was sown" (13:23). New Testament scholar Simon Kistemaker noted that the focus of the parable is not on the seed that was lost—rather, "The farmer looked forward to a harvest when he would bring in the crop. An average yield in those days could be less than ten percent. Should he get returns of thirtyfold, or still more favorable sixtyfold, he would have a bumper crop."[1]

Here we have the assurance that if our hearts and lives are receptive, the Word of God will bear fruit. It is also important to note that in this story, God is continually sowing seed. This parable extends beyond the moment of conversion to speak of a fruitful life, year in and year out:

1. Simon Kistemaker, *The Parables: Understanding the Stories Jesus Told* (Grand Rapids: Baker Books, 2002), 32.

22

"Whoever has will be given more, and they will have an abundance" (13:12a).

Thus, the call of Christ is to keep the soil fresh—to guard our hearts from shallow commitments and crowded days that threaten to choke out the fruit of the Spirit. Good seed requires good soil in order to bear fruit.

John & Kathy
Jerry & Shirley
Jim & Sharon
David
Rita
Betty

# 2

# THE PARABLE OF THE PRODIGAL SON

Luke 15:11–32

## The Story

There was a man who had two sons. The younger one said to his father, "Father, give me my share of the estate." So he divided his property between them.

Not long after that, the younger son got together all he had, set off for a distant country and there squandered his wealth in wild living. After he had spent everything, there was a severe famine in that whole country, and he began to be in need. So he went and hired himself out to a citizen of that country, who sent him to his fields to feed pigs. He longed to fill his stomach with the pods that the pigs were eating, but no one gave him anything.

When he came to his senses, he said, "How many of my father's hired servants have food to spare, and here I am starving to death! I will set out and go back to my father and say to him: Father, I have sinned against heaven and against you. I am no longer worthy to be called your son; make me like one of your hired servants." So he got up and went to his father.

But while he was still a long way off, his father saw him and was filled with compassion for him; he ran to his son, threw his arms around him and kissed him.

The son said to him, "Father, I have sinned against heaven and against you. I am no longer worthy to be called your son."

But the father said to his servants, "Quick! Bring the best robe and put it on him. Put a ring on his finger and sandals on his feet. Bring the fattened calf and kill it. Let's have a feast and celebrate. For this son of mine was dead and is alive again; he was lost and is found." So they began to celebrate.

—Luke 15:11–24

This story of a foolish boy and a forgiving father could end here and be a great story. However, the story continues:

Meanwhile, the older son was in the field. When he came near the house, he heard music and dancing. So he called one of the servants and asked him what was going on. "Your brother has come," he replied, "and your father has killed the fattened calf because he has him back safe and sound."

The older brother became angry and refused to go in. So his father went out and pleaded with him. But he answered his father, "Look! All these years I've been slaving for you and never disobeyed your orders. Yet you never gave me even a young goat so I could celebrate with my friends. But when this son of yours who has squandered your property with prostitutes comes home, you kill the fattened calf for him!"

"My son," the father said, "you are always with me, and everything I have is yours. But we had to celebrate and be glad, because this brother of yours was dead and is alive again; he was lost and is found."

—Luke 15:25–32

## The Window

Even those who know next to nothing about the Bible know something of this story. Its themes and language have been incorporated into the wider culture. For example, Shakespeare borrowed motifs and plot points from this parable and adapted them in *The Merchant of Venice* and *Henry IV*. Composer Arthur Sullivan used the exact language of this text as the basis for one of his fine oratorios, and Benjamin Britten turned the story into an opera. The world's great art museums are filled with works featuring scenes from this drama, and its themes have been woven into contemporary music ranging from country to rap to rock.

Charles Dickens famously called it the greatest short story ever written. And it is a great story, both in terms of its literary craft and its enduring meaning and impact. The plot is simple enough for a child to follow yet profound enough to be the subject of several book-length studies. Scholars have spent centuries poring over this text line by line.

Of all the parables told by Jesus, this is the most richly detailed, dramatic, and personal. It brims with emotions ranging from sadness to triumph to shock and, finally, to an unsettling wish for more. It is, perhaps, the greatest five minutes of storytelling ever. Geraint Vaughan Jones describes it as a story "infused with a transforming vision."[1]

This mini-drama is memorable on many levels. As the story unfolds, the focus shifts from one character to another, building in intensity as it progresses. The younger son is the focus at the beginning; the father takes center stage at the magnificent moment of reconciliation; finally, the focus shifts to the elder brother's response, which unsettles the story's end and leaves the reader wanting more.

With each movement, the plot takes a surprising turn. The image of a boy who becomes so desperately hungry that he scavenges husks from pig slop would be particularly surprising and offensive to Jesus's Jewish audience, since pigs are unclean according to Levitical law. This part of the story reminds us that our choices have consequences—a lesson that too many people learn the hard way.

Another thing that makes this tale unforgettable is the poignancy of the father's response to his son: "But while he was still a long way off, his father saw him and was filled with compassion for him; he ran to his son, threw his arms around him and kissed him" (15:20). What a picture of love and grace—what a portrait of God the Father. Who wouldn't be moved by that kind of love and forgiveness?

The eldest son remains unmoved, apparently—he is the third character to take center stage, and he is unfazed by his father's love. In fact, he clearly resents both his brother and his father. The older brother bristles and protests at the elaborate welcome extended to his wayward brother. He refuses to join the party. The father goes to his older son, just as he went to meet his younger son. The father clearly loves both. However, the elder brother refuses to accept his father's grace.

1. Geraint Vaughan Jones, *The Art and Truth of the Parables* (London: SPCK, 1964), 167.

As New Testament scholar Mark Allan Powell writes, this interaction represents "one of the greatest instances of unresolved conflict in all literature."[2] It demonstrates that someone can be just as rebellious and self-centered inwardly as the prodigal son was outwardly. Thus, the parable of the prodigal son is not just a warm and fuzz,y feel-good story; it also conveys a troubling warning.

This parable is interesting and richly textured; however, its primary purpose is not to entertain but to instruct. This story is the third of a trilogy in Luke 15, which begins with the story of a lost sheep: "Suppose one of you has a hundred sheep and loses one of them. Doesn't he leave the ninety-nine in the open country and go after the lost sheep until he finds it?" (v. 4). The second part of the trilogy is the brief story of a lost coin: "Suppose a woman has ten silver coins and loses one. Doesn't she light a lamp, sweep the house and search carefully until she finds it?" (v. 8). Finally, it is after these two stories that we find the story of the lost son.

A key phrase in this parable, the turning point of the story, is found in verse 17. The phrase appears after the son has taken his inheritance, gone his own way, and finally lost it all. The verse begins with the words, "When he came to his senses . . ." Other translations say, "when he came to himself."

There is a moment in each of our lives when we must come to our senses, or come to ourselves. It means seeing ourselves as we really are—not as we pretend to be, or want to be, or once were. A moment like that can happen in a church service, while reading Scripture, or during meditation on spiritual things—suddenly, the light comes on and we come to our senses. To "come to ourselves" means to accept ourselves and our situations as they really are—only then can we start the journey home.

## The Mirror

Where are you in the story?

The younger son thought he had it all figured out. He perceived that if he just had enough money and distance to be free from home, his life would be filled with pleasure. And it was—for a time. But then

2. Mark Allan Powell, *What is Narrative Criticism? (Guides to Biblical Scholarship New Testament Series)* (Minneapolis: Fortress Press, 1990), 44.

his time ran out—then he had nothing. This boy had everything in the world going for him, but he couldn't see it until he had squandered it all.

Of course, the good news is that he came to his senses. Fortunately, unlike the prodigal son, we don't have to wait until our lives are ruined to come to our senses. We don't have to learn every lesson the hard way. There is a better way—God's way.

If you want to know how God feels about you, just look at the father in this story. Was he angry? Was he set on punishing the son upon his return? No. The father in the story—your heavenly Father—loves you so much that nothing can separate you from his love and forgiveness.

When I was fifteen, I ran away from home. It still embarrasses me to think about it, but some incidental disagreement with my folks made me think I was old enough to strike out on my own. I had about forty-five dollars saved up from mowing lawns, which seemed like a lot of money at the time. So after school, with that money burning a hole in my pocket and an adolescent rebellion stirring in my mind, I bought a bus ticket from my little town in western Ohio to Dayton. From there I bought a ticket to Indianapolis. When I boarded that bus to Indianapolis, I realized I had made a mistake. But how could I go back?

It was almost midnight by the time I reached Indianapolis. There was no one to meet me, no place to stay, and my forty-five dollars had dwindled down to twenty-something.

I hadn't come home from school, and my parents had no idea where I was. Finally, about midnight, I called them from a pay phone. That conversation is still burned into my mind:

"Where are you?"
"Indianapolis."
"How did you get there?"
"On the bus."
"Are you okay?"
"Yes—no. I want to come home."
"Sure."

After talking with my parents, I bought a bus ticket back to Dayton. A few hours later, when I stepped off the bus in the wee hours of the morning, my mother and father were waiting for me. It was my mother who set the tone. There were no harsh words or stern looks—instead, there was rejoicing, hugs, and kisses. It wasn't what I deserved, but it was what I needed. It was a moment of grace.

God waits for us and receives us in the same way. By his grace we are saved—we don't deserve it, and we cannot earn it. It can't be acquired by buying, bartering, or begging. Like fifteen-year-old runaway me, we learn about grace by being graced.

Years ago, the Russian composer Sergei Prokofiev wrote a beautiful orchestral score called *The Prodigal*. After the score made its way to the West, famed choreographer George Balanchine made the music into a ballet and cast the great Russian dancer Mikhail Baryshnikov in the lead role. The result was a stunning performance.

The ballet begins with bright, cheerful music as the father and two sons enter. The dancers' movements communicate joy and love. Then, slowly, the music begins to shift to a more somber tone. Little by little, one of the sons moves away from his father and brother. Slowly, the lights dim on the father and older brother, and by the time the scene ends, the son is at the far end of the stage, surrounded by new friends. The music is dissonant, filled with a cacophony of minor chords.

In the next scene, the boy is all alone. His friends are gone, the music has ended, and the light around him has lost its luster. He lies on the stage, a broken young man. Then, appearing to remember better days, he turns his head and looks back toward the place where he last saw his father.

The music returns with a low, slow cadence, and the son begins to drag himself back across the stage, toward home. When he is about halfway there, his father appears in a bright robe, gazing into the distance in hopes of seeing his son.

Finally, the son draws near, crawling on all fours until he is close enough to touch his father. He reaches out, takes hold of his father's ankles, and draws himself closer; then he grasps his father's knees and raises himself up. Finally, the son takes hold of his father's arms and shoulders and lifts himself into his father's embrace. The light brightens, and the music turns sweet and calm.

It is a beautiful image—but it's wrong! This image in the ballet does not reflect the image in the parable. In the parable, the father does not stand in stoic silence as if to say, "If you can crawl your way back to me—if you can raise yourself up by your own strength—then I'll receive you." No! Jesus paints a portrait of a father who, the moment he sees his son in the distance, runs to him, embraces him, and welcomes him back.

## Conclusion

Written in 1936, "The Capital of the World" is one of Ernest Hemingway's lesser-known short stories. The protagonist of the story is a young boy named Paco, who, after a disagreement with his father, leaves his home village for the romance and glamour of Madrid. In an attempt to find his son, the father follows him to Madrid. Knowing he has little chance of finding Paco by wandering the streets of the city, the father puts an advertisement in the local newspaper, *El Liberal.* The ad reads, "Paco, meet me at the Hotel Montana at noon on Tuesday. All is forgiven! Love, Papa."

At the appointed meeting time, the father is unprepared for what he finds. Paco is an incredibly common name in Spain—and at noon on Tuesday, 800 young men of the same name show up to wait for their fathers, and for the forgiveness they long to receive.[3] The story reminds us that deep within each of our hearts, there is a desire to hear those words: "All is forgiven! Love, Papa."

The parable of the prodigal son is a story of extravagant grace, as seen in the person of the waiting, forgiving father. The father did not require repayment from his son, nor ask for a guarantee that he would never fail again. What grace!

How eager God is to meet wayward daughters and sons—the God who acts not out of anger but compassion. Dorothy Sayers notes, "Like the Father of the Prodigal Son, God can see repentance coming a great way off and is there to meet it."[4] Be assured that once you come to your senses and take the bus home, God is there. And as surely as my mother and father threw their arms of love around me, God will do the same for you.

Like many of Jesus's other parables, this story reminds us that it is God who takes the initiative toward us—like a loving parent who runs to meet a prodigal son, or an employer who pays eleventh-hour workers the same wage as the first-hour crew. He is the God who goes into the highways and byways of this world to invite undeserving guests to his banquet. I am one of those guests. Are you?

---

3. Ernest Hemingway, *The Complete Stories of Ernest Hemingway* (New York: Charles Scribner's Sons, 1987), 29.

4. Dorothy Sayers, "Forgiveness and the Enemy," *The Fortnightly,* vol. 149, no. 892, April 1941, 15.

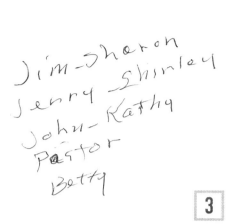

Jim - Sharon
Jerry - Shirley
John - Kathy
Pastor
Betty

## 3

# THE PARABLE OF THE GOOD SAMARITAN

Luke 10:25-37

### The Story

On one occasion an expert in the law stood up to test Jesus. "Teacher," he asked, "what must I do to inherit eternal life?"

"What is written in the Law?" he replied. "How do you read it?"

He answered, "'Love the Lord your God with all your heart and with all your soul and with all your strength and with all your mind'; and, 'Love your neighbor as yourself.'"

"You have answered correctly," Jesus replied. "Do this and you will live."

But he wanted to justify himself, so he asked Jesus, "And who is my neighbor?"

In reply Jesus said: "A man was going down from Jerusalem to Jericho, when he was attacked by robbers. They stripped him of his clothes, beat him and went away, leaving him half dead. A priest happened to be going down the same road, and when he saw the man, he passed by on the other side. So too, a Levite, when he came to the place and saw him, passed by on the other side. But a Samaritan, as he traveled, came where the man was; and when he saw him, he took pity on him. He went to him and bandaged his wounds, pouring on oil and wine.

Then he put the man on his own donkey, brought him to an inn and took care of him. The next day he took out two denarii and gave them to the innkeeper. 'Look after him,' he said, 'and when I return, I will reimburse you for any extra expense you may have.'

"Which of these three do you think was a neighbor to the man who fell into the hands of robbers?"

The expert in the law replied, "The one who had mercy on him." Jesus told him, "Go and do likewise."

—Luke 10:25–37

## The Window

This is one of Jesus's most poignant and powerful parables. It has inspired acts of kindness throughout the globe; hundreds of hospitals, clinics, compassionate ministry centers, and other places of refuge are named for it. The story of the Good Samaritan has come to represent applied Christianity. But while applied faith is a dominant theme in the story, this description falls short of the full meaning.

There is more to the story than a clarion call to charity—it also speaks to religious and cultural prejudice. Though racial tension and hatred form the backdrop of this story, they are overcome by the call to see other people—all people—as our neighbors.

As we approach this story, it's worth noting that it's actually *two* stories. The first story is about the setting and circumstances of Jesus's teaching: "On one occasion an expert in the law stood up to test Jesus" (v. 25). The second story, of course, is the parable itself. The stories are obviously related, but nonetheless, they deal with two different themes. The first story centers on the quest for eternal life; the second focuses on kingdom behavior.

The parable begins with a question from an expert in the law: "What must I do to inherit eternal life?" (v. 25). Although the expert's motive here is to "test" Jesus, the question is vitally important—in fact, it's the most important question we can ask. In the story that follows, the lawyer who seeks to test Jesus is himself put the test.

In response to the inquiry, Jesus answers with a question of his own: "What is written in the law?" (v. 26). Notice that Jesus does not ask, "What do you think?" or, "What do others tell you?" Instead, he appeals to Scripture. The lawyer responds, "'Love the Lord your God with all your heart and with all your soul and with all your strength and with all your mind'; and, 'Love your neighbor as yourself'" (v. 27). The first quote in the lawyer's response is from Deuteronomy 6:5, and the second is from Leviticus 19:18. Together, they summarize all of God's law.

Jesus acknowledges the correctness of the answer, adding, "Do this and you will live" (Luke 10:28). But the lawyer is not satisfied; he presses on, asking, "And who is my neighbor?" (v. 29). Now the stage is set. Those listening lean in to hear Jesus's response: the parable, followed by Jesus's own question.

The first three sentences of the story introduce three characters: a man who had been beaten and robbed by thieves; a priest; and a Levite. Jesus's audience was well aware of the dangers that could befall a lone traveler. And while they may have wondered why the priest and Levite did not stop, they expected the rescuer to be another Jew—perhaps not a religious leader, but a devout man nonetheless.

The two men who passed by the wounded man were religious, like the expert in the law who Jesus was addressing, yet they walked by. Some scholars suggest that the priest and the Levite refused to help the wounded stranger for fear of ritual impurity; coming into contact with a corpse could render them ceremonially impure.

This may have been a factor, but it is also possible, and perhaps more likely, that the two travelers were simply afraid—afraid of thieves who might still be lurking, but also afraid of what helping the man might cost them in terms of time and money. They may have seen the man, but they did not see him as a neighbor; they were blinded by their narrow application of the divine imperative.

As the fourth sentence unfolds, the story takes an unexpected turn. Jesus begins to speak of a Samaritan who is also passing by. His listeners would have expected the Samaritan to not only pass by, but perhaps also inflict more harm upon the wounded traveler. There was no one the Jews despised more than the Samaritans. They were considered both racially and religiously inferior, and Jews would go to great lengths to avoid any contact with them.

However, to the listeners' surprise, Jesus portrayed the Samaritan as the heroic figure in the story. In contrast to the priest and Levite, the Samaritan not only saw the wounded man, but stopped to care for him. Unlike the other travelers, the Samaritan did not ask, "If I stop to help him, what will happen to me?" Instead, he asked, "If I do not stop to help, what will happen to him?" The Samaritan's response conveys both courage and compassion.

Here we encounter the power of the parable. It is the Samaritan, whom the Jews looked down upon, who comes to the rescue. The

Good Samaritan story calls us to see others—to notice those in need, and those whom we might otherwise pass by.

Furthermore, the Samaritan's response goes well beyond what Jesus's audience would have anticipated. He not only stops to help, but also takes the man to an inn, pays for his care, and promises to return and reimburse the innkeeper for any additional expenses. His response demonstrates that loving our neighbor is on ongoing commitment.

At the end of this story, Jesus asks the expert in the law a penetrating question: "Which of these three do you think was a neighbor to the man who fell into the hands of robbers?" (v. 36).

The lawyer may have choked on his answer, but he was honest enough to concede the point. He replies, "The one who had mercy on him" (v. 37).

It is at that point that Jesus declares, "Go and do likewise" (v. 37).

## The Mirror

Some years ago, I studied at Harvard University as a post-doctoral resident fellow. While I was there, I participated in the weekly Charles Merrill Fellowship seminar. At the end of the semester, our small group was invited to the Harvard Faculty club for lunch and a lively discussion. Our host was Charles Merrill of the investment firm Merrill Lynch. It was his family who had established the fellowship and funded our studies at Harvard.

Merrill arrived in Cambridge to meet us just after America had declared war on Iraq following Iraq's invasion of Kuwait. At the time, the Harvard community was up in arms at the thought of the United States going to war.

At one point in our conversation, Merrill asked us to respond to a question: "Tell me what you would say to your congregation on the Sunday after the US invades Kuwait." One by one, my handful of fellow "fellows" responded by saying things like, "I would speak on the words of Jesus, 'Blessed are the peacemakers,' or, 'I would speak of a kingdom where the lion lies down with the lamb.'" Each of my colleagues felt sincerely moved to speak about American hubris, against the use of violence, how this was just a war about oil, and so on.

I understood their points of view, but when it came my turn to respond, I said that I would speak of the parable of the good Samaritan, with special attention to the question Jesus asked: "Which of these three do you think was a neighbor to the man who fell into the hands of robbers?" I asked, "Does this story apply to us as a nation? Can we turn away from the one who fell among thieves?" My friends were religious and zealous, but did they see the people of Kuwait as their neighbors?

On the day I was installed as a university president, a friend gave me a framed keepsake. At the top was a copy of the invitation to my inauguration ceremony; at the bottom was an extended quote from Pulitzer Prize-winning author, physician, and social scientist Robert Coles, out of *Harvard Diary: Reflections on the Sacred and the Secular*. In one section, Coles describes an interview he had with a young woman who had been mistreated in her job at the university:

> She gradually began to realize how much she had learned without question, the hard way. She began to realize that being clever, brilliant, even what gets called "well-educated" is not to be equated, necessarily, with being considerate, kind, tactful, even plain polite or civil. She began to realize that one's proclaimed social or political views—however articulately humanitarian—are not always guarantors of one's everyday behavior. One can write lofty editorials (or "diary" entries!) and falter badly in one's moral life. One can speak big-hearted words, write incisive and thoughtful prose—and be a rather crude, arrogant, smug person in the course of getting through a day. In this regard, I remember a Nicaraguan commandante speaking noble and egalitarian thoughts to my sons and me in Managua—and meanwhile, my son noticed, he pressed buttons, secretaries came and went, bringing coffee, and never were they acknowledged, let alone thanked.
>
> Character, my father used to tell me, is what you're like when no one's watching you—or, I guess, when you forget that others are watching. Dickens, as usual, was shrewd about this sort of irony in our lives—a tragedy, really, for us—when he used the expression "telescopic philanthropy" in *Bleak House* to describe what the student quoted above had witnessed: someone whose compassion for far-off South Africa's black people was boundless (and eagerly announced to others through the act of writing) but who could also, near at home, behave toward another person as shamelessly as any South African bureaucrat might contrive to act.
>
> No wonder Jesus spent his short time with us doing those everyday acts of charity, offering those small gestures, emphasizing the importance of the concrete deed—the pastoral life. Let those of us who find that words come easy, and who like to play with ideas, and call the

attention of others to our words and ideas, beware. Our jeopardy is real and continuing.[1]

Coles's references here to "everyday acts of charity" and "the importance of the concrete deed" strike a chord with the parable at hand. Russian novelist Leo Tolstoy is known for such classic works as *War and Peace* and *Anna Karenina,* but he also wrote essays and short stories. One of his best short stories, "Two Old Men," tells of two men named Efim and Elisha who decide they want to make a pilgrimage to Jerusalem before they die. The journey will be long, and they have only modest means, so they decide to walk.

The old men have been walking for about five weeks when they happen upon a small hut. Elisha wants to stop to get some water, so Efim goes on with the promise that Elisha will soon follow. As Elisha draws near to the house, he sees a gaunt figure lying near the door. When Elisha calls to him, the man does not respond. When he enters the hut, Elisha finds two women and two small children, all weak from starvation nearly to the point of death. Rather than catch up with Efim immediately, Elisha decides to share his bread and care for the people in the hut.

As the story unfolds, Elisha remains in the village, helping the residents regain their health and begin to live again. He never makes it to Jerusalem, and eventually returns home.

Efim completes the pilgrimage to Jerusalem but is disappointed. He visits the holy sites but is not moved. He waits for Elisha, but he never arrives. Efim decides to retrace his steps across the continent and make his way back to Russia.

Eventually, Efim arrives in a village that seems familiar. He quickly realizes this is where he left his friend—however, the village seems different now. The streets are filled with people working or playing; there are livestock and crops.

"What happened here?" Efim asks someone passing by. The villager tells him that a man stopped among them and restored them to life.

The story ends with the friends' reunion in their homeland, each recalling his separate journey. The last line of the story is this: "But he [Efim] now understood that the best way to keep one's vows to God and to do His will, is for each man while he lives to show love and do

---

1. Robert Coles, *Harvard Diary: Reflections on the Sacred and the Secular* (New York: Crossroads Publishing Company, 1988), 111.

good to others."[2] In the same way, the parable of the good Samaritan calls us to take responsibility for those in need.

## Conclusion

Throughout Jesus's teachings, as well as the rest of the New Testament, we see that the defining characteristic of God's kingdom is love. God wants his love to flow through us, even to the point of loving our enemies. It's easy to love those who love us and those who are like us—but that is not the test of genuine, Christlike love. This parable demonstrates that the command to "love your neighbor as yourself" (Leviticus 19:18) extends to anyone in need. The Samaritan sacrificed his time and money to care for a stranger. And we, too, are to "go and do likewise" (Luke 10:37).

2. Leo Tolstoy, *Two Old Men* (Washington, DC: The Trinity Forum, 1991), 31.

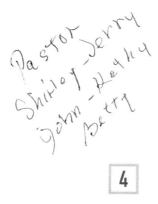

Pastor Jerry
Shirley - Kathy
John - Betty

# 4

# THE PARABLE OF THE WORKERS IN THE VINEYARD

### The Story

The kingdom of heaven is like a landowner who went out early in the morning to hire workers for his vineyard. He agreed to pay them a denarius for the day and sent them into his vineyard.

About nine in the morning he went out and saw others standing in the marketplace doing nothing. He told them, "You also go and work in my vineyard, and I will pay you whatever is right." So they went.

He went out again about noon and about three in the afternoon and did the same thing. About five in the afternoon he went out and found still others standing around. He asked them, "Why have you been standing here all day long doing nothing?"

"Because no one has hired us," they answered.

He said to them, "You also go and work in my vineyard."

When evening came, the owner of the vineyard said to his foreman, "Call the workers and pay them their wages, beginning with the last ones hired and going to the first."

The workers who were hired about five in the afternoon came and each received a denarius. So when those came who were hired first, they expected to receive more. But each of them also received a denarius.

41

When they received it, they began to grumble against the landowner. "These who were hired last worked only one hour," they said, "and you have made them equal to us who have borne the burden of the work and the heat of the day."

But he answered one of them, "I am not being unfair to you, friend. Didn't you agree to work for a denarius? Take your pay and go. I want to give the one who was hired last the same as I gave you. Don't I have the right to do what I want with my own money? Or are you envious because I am generous?"

So the last will be first, and the first will be last.

(Matthew 20:1–16)

## The Window

This story marks one of the kingdom parables recorded by Matthew. The story is divided into two main sections: 1) the hiring, and 2) the payment of the workers. However, unlike the parable of the good Samaritan, this parable does not end with the message, "Go and do likewise" (Luke 10:37). The focus of the story is not on paying fair wages or treating everyone equally; rather, the purpose of the story is to provide a portrait of God who freely gives good gifts to all. When we look through the "window" of this parable, we see a portrait of grace.

In this story, the workday begins early, perhaps at sunrise, and laborers gather to wait for the landowner to come and offer work. Working as a day laborer (as many people still do today) is not an easy existence, for work is more than a means of supporting ourselves. At its best, work gives dignity and meaning to life. This is why, when people go long periods of time without finding work, their sense of identity and self-worth can be eroded.

At first light, the landowner enlists a set of workers and agrees upon a set wage of one denarius. The workers then make their way to the vineyard. Around 9:00 a.m., the landowner sees others standing idle in the marketplace and offers them work. They too enter the vineyard to work. There seems to be plenty of work to go around, for this scene is repeated throughout the day; every three hours, the landowner returns to the town square and hires additional workers. The work goes on until about 6:00 p.m.

At first reading, we might focus on the workers as the central characters. However, the landlord is actually the central figure of this story. He is the one who visits the marketplace at dawn, hires the workers,

42

notices the need for more laborers, and repeatedly returns for still more workers. It is he who instructs his steward to pay each worker the same wage, and it is he who addresses those who think they were mistreated. The owner of the vineyard is the driving figure of the story from beginning to end, and it is he to whom Jesus compares the kingdom of heaven in Matthew 20:1.

At the end of the day, the owner sends his steward out to pay the laborers. The steward first pays those who were hired at the end of the day; the ones who were hired at the beginning of the day are last in line. Every laborer, no matter how long he had worked, received the same amount: one day's wage, a denarius.

When they saw that those who had worked only part of the day also received a denarius, the other workers, some who had been there all day, assumed they would be paid more. However, everyone received the same amount. Those who worked all day complained, "These who were hired last worked only one hour," they said, "and you have made them equal to us who have borne the burden of the work and the heat of the day" (v. 12).

At first glance, this seems unfair; it certainly defies modern labor practices. However, the parable illustrates something beyond fair wages for a day's labor. Jesus is pulling back the curtain to reveal a glimpse of the kingdom, where people are not judged on works or merit. We may think it's unjust that those who work only a short time receive the same reward as those who work all day, but God's thoughts are not our thoughts.

When some of the workers complain, the landowner gently replies, "I am not being unfair to you, friend. Didn't you agree to work for a denarius? Take your pay and go. I want to give to the one who was hired last the same as I gave you. Don't I have the right to do what I want with my own money? Or are you envious because I am generous? So the last will be first, and the first will be last" (vv. 13–16). The NKJV adds to verse 16, "For many are called, but few chosen."

Each laborer had agreed to work for what the vineyard owner would pay. Those who began in the morning accepted the offer of a denarius as fair and appropriate, so no one has the right to complain about what they've been given. What the landowner gives to others is outside their agreement.

The message of the parable is simple yet profound: God is generous and gracious to all. Those who are called at the "eleventh hour" have just as much access to God's kingdom as those called earlier. The parable also underscores the sovereignty of God, echoing one of his Old-Testament declarations: "I will have mercy on whom I will have mercy, and I will have compassion on whom I will have compassion" (Exodus 33:19).

## The Mirror

Grace is at the heart of the gospel. Paul put it like this: "For by grace you have been saved through faith, and that not of yourselves; it is the gift of God, not of works, lest anyone should boast" (Ephesians 2:8–9, NKJV).

Is there a richer or stranger idea than grace? The only word that comes close is its cousin, "love," yet grace is arguably more intriguing. Love is often reciprocal; we love those who love us. We love those we like and those who are like us.

Grace, on the other hand, is indiscriminate. Grace is totally undeserved. Grace comes free to people who do not deserve it. Grace isn't fair.

I had a wonderful mother who died far too young. I think about her often; she was a gift of grace to me. My mother lived her life between two of the lines of "Amazing Grace." The first of those two lines is this: "'Tis grace hath brought me safe thus far."

My mother's name was Betty Jean Bowling—except that wasn't her name. Bowling was her married name, but her given name was not Betty Jean. Her real name was Vera Leona—but we did not know it, and neither did she.

My mother didn't learn her real name until she was in her thirties, when she needed a copy of her birth certificate. When she contacted the county clerk's office, they told her that they had no record of her birth. She assured them that she had definitely been born. Eventually, after a little more digging, the county clerk's office found a record of a daughter born to my mother's parents about a month after her birth date—but the name on the birth certificate was Vera Leona.

What happened was this: My mother was born into a good family, but by the time she was born as the last of seven children, things had gotten tough. Her mother died shortly after she was born.

Apparently, a relative promised to stop by the county seat to file my mother's birth certificate on one of his trips into town. However, it was several weeks before he made it to the courthouse, and by then, he could not remember which name the parents had chosen. He liked the name Vera Leona, so that's what he entered on her birth certificate.

My mother grew up during the Great Depression, and her father, like many other men, had to leave home to find work. They lived in eastern Kentucky, but he ended up working in Cleveland, Ohio, for many years. He would visit home for a few days every other weekend.

As a result, my mother was raised by her older siblings. Life was tough. She didn't have a mother and didn't really have a home; but in the midst of all that upheaval, she found the Lord, and my father found her.

Almost immediately after my mother and father were married, he left with the army to fight in World War II and was gone for more than two years. But after the war, they started life over together. And because my mother never really had a home growing up, she worked hard to make sure our family would—and we did. I tell people that my childhood was similar to the old *Leave It to Beaver* television show—a mom, dad, and two sons living the American dream. That was my world as a kid.

Why should I have been born into such a home and be raised under the influence and nurture of such a woman? Did I deserve the gift of such a loving, tender, strong, humble, confident, generous, frugal, funny, kind, and gracious mother? No. My mother was a gift of grace, unmerited and undeserved. I saw grace in her, and she understood grace in a personal way: "'Tis grace hath brought me safe thus far / And grace will lead me home."

My mother's experience of God's grace early in her life gave her confidence that grace would lead her home. Because my mother understood grace, she became a gracious person.

What is grace? Grace is the English translation of the Latin term *gratia*, itself a translation of the Greek word *charis*, which means "gift." Grace is a gift set against a backdrop of Hebrew words like compassion, care, kindness, and long-suffering. God looks with favor upon you. In spite of all your faults and failures, he has nothing but your best interests at heart.

In the New Testament, the word "grace" is of central importance. It is the keyword of Christianity. Grace is what the gospel is all about, for we are saved by grace through faith. Thomas Oden writes, "Grace is God's way of empowering the bound will and healing the suffering spirit. The unmerited blessing of God is being offered to all who are alienated from their true selves."[1] It is a spiritual energy.

The human race is remarkably resourceful in attempting to find substitutes for grace. We place our trust in things, in power, in reputation, in our common intellect. But no matter how much we have, who we are, or what we know, we can never gain nor merit what is freely given by God.

God is gracious not because of who we are, but because of who he is. God is love and love must be expressed. It's by grace that we are objects of his love. We are broken, and grace alone is the glue. Morality cannot mend us; personality will not fix the problem; education cannot restore what's been broken; prosperity has no power to restore humanity. Grace alone is the glue.

The attraction of grace is that it's something we can never get—it can only be given to us. We cannot earn it, deserve it, or bring it about. We can only receive it and be thankful. Grace is God's undeserved favor, his unmerited love. Shauna Niequist describes it this way: "Grace isn't about having a second chance; grace is having so many chances that you could use them through all eternity and never come up empty. It's when you finally realize that the other shoe isn't going to drop, ever."[2]

Frederick Buechner suggests that grace is the "crucial eccentricity" of the Christian faith. As such, grace is God acting in spontaneous goodness to save sinners—loving the unlovely. Though we have nothing within us to merit God's favor, he favors us nonetheless. As the opening chapter of the Gospel of John tells us, "Out of his fullness we have all received grace in place of grace already given" (1:16).

If you are buying a house and have a mortgage with a bank, your payments are probably due on the first of each month. However, should you fail to make a payment on that date, you may have until the 15th to send it in before receiving a penalty. This extra time is called a "grace period."

Christians also have a grace period, but it's different from what the bank extends to its mortgage holders. The bank system is not grace in the full sense of the term; it is merely a temporary reprieve. The bank's favor comes to an end on the 15th. They will then demand full payment or add a penalty.

1. Thomas C. Oden, *The Transforming Power of Grace* (Nashville: Abingdon Press, 1993), 68.

2. Niequist, *Bittersweet*, 83.

By contrast, the debt for our sins has been fully paid by Jesus's death on the cross; as Romans 5:20 says, "But where sin abounded, grace abounded much more" (NKJV). Furthermore, God, by his Spirit, gives us both the desire and the strength to do his will. That makes our lives a continuous extension of divine favor, which we appropriate by faith: "So then, just as you have received Christ Jesus as Lord, continue to live in him" (Colossians 2:6, CSB).

Every day is a grace period on the receiving end of God's unending favor. It calls us to live in a way that brings glory to God.

Jesus had a lot to say about grace, and he said most of it through parables. Some of his parables, including the story of the workers in the vineyard, are designed to teach us about grace and the character of God. Grace cannot be reduced to generally acceptable accounting principles. None of us gets paid according to merit; if the world could have been saved by good bookkeeping, it would have been saved by Moses, not Jesus. It would have come down to keeping all the commandments.

Grace does not rest on merit or performance, which means grace really is not fair—but that, of course, is the point. If it were fair—if everyone got what he or she deserved—where would we be? No one could find favor in God's sight. So he throws the whole idea of merit as a prerequisite out the windows and substitutes grace.

This is a hard thing for us to grasp. Our world operates on a different economy—one that says, "It can be yours if you buy it or earn it or deserve it in some way." Therefore, we naturally assume that we have to *do* something in order to be accepted by God. In this context, grace sounds a startling note of contradiction and freedom.

As such, grace carries with it a life-changing power: it is transformative. How do you suppose the prodigal son thought of his father after such a moment of grace? I'm convinced that it changed him and changed his relationship with everyone else.

Think of the thief on the cross. He was a career criminal—his death sentence speaks to the seriousness of his crimes. Yet, at the last moment of his life, he experiences a moment of grace. In response to his simple, sincere prayer—"Jesus, remember me when you come into your kingdom"—his guilt was swept away and he received the promise, "today you will be with me in paradise" (Luke 23:42–43). Grace overcomes all things: sin, indifference, human limitation and failures. Grace stands outside the rules; it's not fair, but that's the point.

## Conclusion

One final note: a unique feature of this parable is that it is preceded and followed immediately by a simple proverb that seems to introduce the story and provide a final explanation. The last sentence of chapter 19 introduces the parable that opens chapter 20. Matthew 19:30 states: "But many who are first will be last, and many who are last will be first." Following the parable comes this verse: "So the last will be first, and the first will be last" (20:16).

This proverbial theme also appears within the parable as the landowner declares, "Call the workers and pay them their wages, beginning with the last ones hired and going on to the first" (Matthew 20:8). This repeated theme, set against the backdrop of this particular story, reinforces the understanding that both the first and the last who enter the kingdom will receive the full benefit of the landlord's generosity. Herein is a picture of grace.

No one can earn or deserve the blessings of the kingdom; these gifts of grace are equally available to all who accept Christ as Savior.

_Jim_
_Sherry_
_Pastor_
_John & Kathy_
_John_
_Betty_

# 5

# THE PARABLE OF
# THE PERSISTENT WIDOW

Luke 18:1-8

## The Story _John_

Then Jesus told his disciples a parable to show them that they should always pray and not give up. He said: "In a certain town there was a judge who neither feared God nor cared what people thought. And there was a widow in that town who kept coming to him with the plea, 'Grant me justice against my adversary.'

"For some time he refused. But finally he said to himself, 'Even though I don't fear God or care what people think, yet because this widow keeps bothering me, I will see that she gets justice, so that she won't eventually come and attack me!'"

And the Lord said, "Listen to what the unjust judge says. And will not God bring about justice for his chosen ones, who cry out to him day and night? Will he keep putting them off? I tell you, he will see that they get justice, and quickly. However, when the Son of Man comes, will he find faith on the earth?"

—Luke 18:1–8

49

## The Window

Have you ever spent time praying for something only to find that nothing seems to happen? Do you ever struggle with God's apparent silence? Do you ever want to give up praying for something because God doesn't seem to be answering?

If you have, you're not alone; most people have experienced seasons when their prayers seem ineffective. Jesus has a parable—two parables, in fact—for just such moments in life.

Luke 11 opens with the following words: "One day Jesus was praying in a certain place. When he finished, one of his disciples said to him, 'Lord, teach us to pray'" (Luke 11:1). In response, Jesus teaches them what we have come to know as the Lord's Prayer. A few verses later, he declares, "Ask and it will be given to you; seek and you will find; knock and the door will be opened to you. For everyone who asks receives; the one who seeks finds; and to the one who knocks, the door will be opened" (Luke 11:9–10).

As a follow-up to his teachings on prayer, Jesus uses a parable to emphasize the importance of prayer, the nature of faith, and the character of God. Though it is sometimes referred to as the parable of the unjust judge, the focus of the story is actually on the widow and her persistence—thus, it's better called the parable of the persistent widow. The same theme appears in the parable of the friend in need.

> Then Jesus said to them, "Suppose you have a friend, and you go to him at midnight and say, 'Friend, lend me three loaves of bread; a friend of mine on a journey has come to me, and I have no food to offer him.' And suppose the one inside answers, 'Don't bother me. The door is already locked, and my children and I are in bed. I can't get up and give you anything.' I tell you, even though he will not get up and give you the bread because of friendship, yet because of your shameless audacity he will surely get up and give you as much as you need.
>
> (Luke 11:5–8)

Because he wants us to know where Jesus is headed with the story, Luke introduces it with a word of commentary: "Then Jesus told his disciples a parable to show them that they should always pray and not give up" (Luke 18:1). The story introduces us to the legal system of the day and to two people at opposite ends of the judicial spectrum—one powerful and one powerless. The judge is the epitome of power;

he "neither feared God nor cared what people thought" (18:2). The widow who enters the courtroom asking for justice, on the other hand, represents the depth of helplessness and weakness. She has no power, no social or political standing. Justice may well be on her side, but she has no leverage.

The judge refuses the widow's request—there's nothing in it for him, and he doesn't care about the widow. However, rather than giving up, the widow "kept coming to him with the plea, 'Grant me justice against my adversary'" (18:3). In this battle of wills, the widow's persistence is her only hope. Finally, the judge relents, saying, "Even though I don't fear God or care what people think, yet because this widow keeps bothering me, I will see that she gets justice, so that she won't eventually come and attack me!" (18:4–5). The judge gives in not out of compassion or a sense of justice, but out of self-interest.

Up to this point, the story is rather unsettling. What is Jesus telling us? Is he saying that if we want God to come to our aid, we have to nag him? Is God a selfish, disinterested judge? Surely not, for as Scripture declares, "the prayer of a righteous person is powerful and effective (James 5:16). Rather, this parable is a story of contrast. The judge does not represent God, and we don't have to wear God down until he finally gives in to our requests. In fact, the point of the story is that God is *not* like the judge: "will not God bring about justice for his chosen ones, who cry out to him day and night? Will he keep putting them off? I tell you, he will see that they get justice, and quickly" (Luke 18:7–8). J. Ellsworth Kalas writes:

> This parable is a powerful reassurance in a world where evil seems sometimes to run rampant. It must have been particularly bracing to the generation that first received copies of Luke's Gospel, for by that time the tiny band of believers was again and again being victimized by persecution. In the midst of attacks by powerful governments that were not overly concerned with justice or fair play, believers were promised that God cared and was at work to set things right.[1]

Beyond providing assurance of God's care, this parable has another message: it encourages us to pray with perseverance, because God will surely hear our petitions and respond. In fact, the parable declares, "he will see that they get justice, and quickly" (18:8). Quickly? What about

---

1. J. Ellsworth Kalas, *Parables of Jesus* (Nashville: Abingdon Press, 1988), 74.

the times when the answers to our prayers seem delayed? This passage reminds us that God's view of time is different than ours; thus, we must learn the spiritual discipline of patience coupled with perseverance.

The fact that the protagonist of the story is a widow is also interesting. Scripture repeatedly reminds us of God's concern for the poor, the stranger, the orphan, and the widow. It also offers examples of widows exercising great faith and determination. Tamar, Ruth, Orpah, Naomi, and others seem to shatter the stereotype of the helpless widow. In the same way, the widow in Jesus's story first appears to fit the stereotype—poor, elderly, frail, and helpless. Yet as the story unfolds, we see strength in her weakness. On the one hand, she is powerless; yet her persistence is what secures her final victory.

## The Mirror

Randy Alcorn recounts the following story about persistence:

> In 1952, young Florence Chadwick stepped into the waters of the Pacific Ocean off Catalina Island, determined to swim to the shore of mainland California. She'd already been the first woman to swim the English Channel both ways. The weather was foggy and chilly; she could hardly see the boats accompanying her. Still, she swam for fifteen hours. When she begged to be taken out of the water along the way, her mother, in a boat alongside, told her she was close and that she could make it. Finally, physically and emotionally exhausted, she stopped swimming and was pulled out. It wasn't until she was on the boat that she discovered the shore was less than half a mile away.
>
> At a news conference the next day she said, "All I could see was the fog....I think if I could have seen the shore, I would have made it."[2]

After his victory over Napoleon at the battle of Waterloo, the Duke of Wellington reportedly said, "My soldiers were not braver than the enemy, but they were brave five minutes longer."[3] There are times when victory comes through persistence. For believers, the antidote to despair is not determination—it is dependence. It is a faith that rests upon

2. Randy Alcorn, "Florence Chadwick and the Fog," Eternal Perspective Ministries, last modified January 21, 2010, https://www.epm.org/resources/2010/Jan/21/florence-chadwick-and-fog/.

3. Gary Inrig, *The Parables: Understanding What Jesus Meant* (Grand Rapids: Discovery House Publishers, 1991), 149.

the deep conviction that God is just, and that God hears and answers our prayers.

In Equatorial Africa, far from any pharmacies or hospitals, a woman died in childbirth, leaving behind a grieving two-year-old daughter and a premature baby in danger of succumbing to the chill of the night. With no incubator, no electricity, and few supplies, the newborn's life was in jeopardy. A helper filled a hot water bottle to provide the warmth the infant so desperately needed, but suddenly, the rubber burst. It was the last hot water bottle in the village.

A visiting missionary physician from Northern Ireland, Dr. Helen Roseveare, asked the orphans to pray for the situation, but a faith-filled ten-year-old named Ruth seemed to go too far.

"Please, God, send us a water bottle," she implored. "It'll be no good tomorrow, God, the baby will be dead; so please send it this afternoon." As if that request was not sufficiently audacious, she added, "And while you are about it, would you please send a dolly for the little girl so she'll know you really love her?"

"I was put on the spot," Roseveare later said. "Could I honestly say, 'Amen'? I just did not believe that God could do this. Oh, yes, I know that he can do everything. The Bible says so, but there are limits, aren't there?" Their only hope of getting a water bottle would be in a parcel sent from Ireland, but Roseveare had never received one during the almost four years she had lived there. "Anyway," she mused, "if anyone did send a parcel, who would put in a hot water bottle? I live on the equator!"

A couple of hours later, a car dropped off a twenty-two-pound package. The orphans helped open it and sort through the contents: some clothing for them, bandages for the leprosy patients, and a bit of food.

Roseveare recalls, "As I put my hand in again, I felt . . . could it really be? I grasped it and pulled it out. Yes! A brand-new rubber hot water bottle! I cried. I had not asked God to send it; I had not truly believed that he could."

With that, little Ruth rushed forward. "If God has sent the bottle, he must have sent the dolly too!" she exclaimed.

She dug through the packaging and found a beautifully dressed doll at the bottom of the parcel. Ruth asked, "Can I go over with you, Mummy, and give this dolly to that little girl, so she'll know that Jesus really loves her?"

The parcel had been packed five months earlier by Roseveare's former Sunday school class. The leader, feeling God's prompting, included the hot water bottle; a little girl contributed the doll. And of course this package, the only one ever to arrive during Roseveare's time in Africa, was delivered the same day Ruth prayed for it with the faith of a child.[4]

That is an example of God's willingness to answer our prayers and his perfect timing in doing so. However, there are other times when answers are delayed and it seems that God has not heard our prayers—and most of the time, we don't know why. It is in those real-life moments that we must learn to trust. We must remember that God's time is not always our timing. The unjust judge delayed his answer out of indifference—God does not.

Just as earthly parents wait to respond to their child's request because they know the timing is wrong or the request isn't in the child's best interest, God may answer in ways we don't expect for our own good. Such delays may be frustrating and painful; yet such moments may also help clarify our needs and desires and deepen our devotion. Delay is not a form of denial, but a means of preparation and spiritual refinement.

In his book *Lion and Lamb: The Relentless Tenderness of Jesus*, Brennan Manning tells the story of a young priest who goes to a new parish. During the priest's first few days in the parish, a young woman comes to the priest and asks if he will call on her sick father. Soon the priest arrives to visit and anoint the old man. As they visit, the priest notices an empty chair pulled close to the head of the bed.

The priest asks if the man had received another visitor. The sick man tells the priest that he had never been able to really pray until a friend explained to him that prayer was a conversation with Jesus. His friend had told him, "Just talk to Jesus as if he were sitting in a chair right there with you. Talk to him and then listen for him to reply."

"So sometimes, father," the man said, "I just pull up the chair and talk to Jesus. But don't tell my daughter—she'll think I am crazy."

About a week later, the daughter told the young priest that her father had died. "He was resting well, so I left him for a couple of hours," she said. "When I got back, he was gone."

"Did he go peacefully?" the priest asked.

"Yes, father . . . but there was one thing. His head was not on the pillow; he had rested it on a chair pulled close to his bedside."[5]

---

4. Helen Roseveare, *Give Me This Mountain* (Glasgow, Scotland: Christian Focus Publications, 2006).

5. Brennan Manning, *Lion and Lamb: The Relentless Tenderness of Jesus* (Grand Rapids: Chosen Books, 1986), 129–130.

The parable of the persistent widow should encourage us to continue in prayer without giving up—not because God is like the heartless judge, but because Jesus assures us that God will respond. Thus, we can pray with confidence. We need not cross our fingers hoping that God is listening. Our standing before God is not like the widow's standing before the judge; God describes us as "his chosen ones" (Luke 18:7). We approach him as children coming to their father. Our persistence in prayer does not change God—it changes us. It builds our confidence.

As a further point of consideration, we might ask if we can see ourselves in the judge. Do we truly fear God? Do we respect, revere, honor, obey, submit to, and follow God? Or like the judge, do our lives say, "God does not weigh heavily in my life; God does not factor heavily in my decision-making; who God is and what God says are not really important to me"?

We should also consider: do we truly care for people—not just in theory, but in practice? The judge sees the woman in need suffering injustice, but does nothing. Someone has sinned against her—a sin of commission—but the judge's sin is a sin of omission. He could render a verdict and bring justice, but he doesn't.

Is there someone you could be helping, serving, or defending, but aren't? It's not enough to value compassion, empathy, love, mercy, respect, and generosity; our lifestyles must embody and demonstrate those values.

If someone were to look at your schedule, would it reveal a real care for people? If they reviewed your budget, would it reveal compassion? Many people who think they are compassionate rarely display it in their daily lives. By definition, that is hypocrisy.

The woman in the story is vulnerable. Her family has not received her; her husband has died; and she has low status under the law. Someone has harmed her, but she cannot afford an attorney to stand before the judge. There is no one to represent her—she is vulnerable. And what does the judge do? He exploits her vulnerability by ignoring her case.

We must ask ourselves: who around us is vulnerable? Many people, whether they are teachers, coaches, parents, pastors, managers, or bosses, have some sort of authority or influence over others. Therefore, we must ask ourselves: when we deal with vulnerable people, do we take them for granted? Exploit them? Or protect them?

## Conclusion

Jesus commended the widow because she persevered even though everything was stacked against her. Her cause was right, but that is not why she won; she prevailed because she did not give up.

The last sentence of the parable is also instructive. In a sense, the point of the parable is not about our persistence in prayer, but about our faith in the midst of delay and injustice. Therefore, Jesus does not end the story with a question. He does not ask, "Will your prayers be answered?" Rather, he concludes with a different question: "When the Son of Man comes, will he find faith on the earth?" (Luke 18:8).

*Shirley*
*Jerry*
*Jim*
*Rita*
*John Kathy*
*Betty*

## 6

# THE PARABLE OF
# COUNTING THE COST

Luke 14:25-35

### The Story

Large crowds were traveling with Jesus, and turning to them he said: "If anyone comes to me and does not hate father and mother, wife and children, brothers and sisters—yes, even their own life—such a person cannot be my disciple. And anyone who does not carry their cross and follow me cannot be my disciple.

"Suppose one of you wants to build a tower. Won't you first sit down and estimate the cost to see if you have enough money to complete it? For if you lay the foundation and are not able to finish it, everyone who sees it will ridicule you, saying, 'This person began to build and wasn't able to finish.'

"Or suppose a king is about to go to war against another king. Won't he first sit down and consider whether he is able with ten thousand men to oppose the one coming against him with twenty thousand? If he is not able, he will send a delegation while the other is still a long way off and will ask for terms of peace. In the same way, those of you who do not give up everything you have cannot be my disciples.

"Salt is good, but if it loses its saltiness, how can it be made salty again? It is fit neither for the soil nor for the manure pile; it is thrown out.

"Whoever has ears to hear, let them hear." (Luke 14:25–35)

## The Window

The twin parables of the person who wanted to build a tower and the king preparing for war are found only in the Gospel of Luke. Jesus told these stories at a time when large crowds were following him, anticipating his ascendance as an earthly ruler—they did not realize that his journey would end at the cross. To counter this misperception, Jesus cautioned his followers, "those of you who do not give up everything you have cannot be my disciples" (14:33).

There are many crosscurrents in these stories, but one thing that recurs is the following phrase: "He cannot be my disciple." Here, rather than recruiting supporters, Jesus seems to be actively discouraging followers. Jesus does not say this to dishearten those who are following him—he is simply warning them to count the cost with two interlocking stories.

William Barclay tells of a moment when Queen Elizabeth of the United Kingdom was a girl—evidently she was forbidden by her parents from doing something she wanted to do. In frustration she said, "I am a princess and I will do what I like!" In response, her grandfather, King George V, responded, "My dear, you are a princess and that is one reason why, all your life, you will never be able to do as you like."[1] Likewise, to follow Jesus is to seek his kingdom first; our ambition must take second place to our commitment to service. Those who choose to follow Christ are blessed, but they must be willing to subordinate their wills to the work of the kingdom.

The context of this story helps provide added insight. Immediately preceding this parable is the parable of the great banquet, which celebrates the gift of God's grace. It reminds us that the kingdom is not reserved for those who meet certain criteria, but for all who will trust in Christ and respond to his invitation to come and dine at his table. However, to complement that grace, we must be wholly committed to the Lord Jesus.

There are people whose relationship to Christ is one of attachment without commitment—Luke tells us that "large crowds were traveling with Jesus" (14:25). Most of these people were curious but not committed. They were interested in what they might get, rather than what they had to give.

---

1. William Barclay, *The Parables of Jesus* (Louisville: Westminster John Knox Press, 1999), 207.

While preparing for his 1914 Imperial Trans-Antarctic Expedition to the South Pole aboard his ship *Endurance*, the explorer Ernest Shackleton ran the following ad in the newspaper: "Men wanted for hazardous journey to South Pole. Small wages, bitter cold, long months of complete darkness, constant danger. Safe return doubtful. Honor and recognition in case of success."[2]

Who would answer such an advertisement? Only those who clearly understood the expectations and dangers of such a commitment. The great explorer knew that he must have men who had counted the cost before they set sail into the unknown. Likewise, Jesus is seeking serious followers whose highest commitment is to him and his coming kingdom.

## The Mirror

Someone once noted that behind every successful man is a surprised mother-in-law. In my case, her name is Doris Cheeseman. Doris, who is now over ninety, is a wonderful woman—bright, generous, kind, and just a little mischievous (in the best sense of the word).

To give you an idea of Doris's sense of humor, I'll tell the story of the time my wife, Jill, went to take her mother to a doctor's appointment.

As they were getting ready, Doris said to Jill, "They're going to ask me how old I am, and I'm not going to tell them."

"That's okay, Mom," Jill replied. "If you don't want to, you don't have to tell them."

"Well, they always ask, and I'm not telling them!"

They went to the appointment.

The doctor and nurse completed the routine exam, but they never asked about Doris's age. So, just as they were wrapping up, Doris said, "Aren't you going to ask me how old I am?"

"Well, how old are you, Mrs. Cheeseman?"

"I'm not telling," Doris replied.

Not long ago, Doris asked Jill how I was doing. Jill told her that I was busy putting the final touches on my baccalaureate message for that year's graduating class. Always wanting to be helpful, my mother-in-law later sent me a joke to include in the message.

2. Carl Hopkins Elmore, *Quit You Like Men* (New York: Charles Scribner's Sons, 1944), 53.

I appreciate humor as much as the next person, but in reality, one cannot just insert a joke into a sermon. It would seem artificial at best. However, what was I to do? On one hand, I had a baccalaureate message, and on the other, an email from my mother-in-law with the following joke included: "Do you know what the hat said to the scarf? You can hang around here somewhere, if you wish, but I'm going on a head."

I was telling a friend of mine this story. He thought about it for a moment and then, in all seriousness, said to me, "You ought to use that."

"What do you mean?" I asked.

He said, "It describes this moment for graduates. They may want to hang around somewhere, but they need to go on ahead."

Therefore, with the help of my mother-in-law and the encouragement of my friend, I spoke to the graduates about Christ's call to go on ahead; to keep moving; to go into all the world and make disciples; to be a disciple; and to live a life worthy of their calling. I told the students, "Don't just hang around somewhere—go on ahead."

Dietrich Bonhoeffer's classic book *The Cost of Discipleship* explores in depth what it means to follow Christ. In doing so, Bonhoeffer makes a distinction between "cheap" and "costly" grace. For him, cheap grace is forgiveness that does not call for genuine repentance; it is "grace without discipleship, grace without the cross, grace without Jesus Christ." For Bonhoeffer, "When Christ calls a man, he bids him come and die."[3]

In this passage, Jesus is claiming priority in all of our relationships; we are to love nothing and no one more than we love him. The purpose of this call is not to denigrate our other relationships, but to elevate our relationship with Christ.

The witness of Scripture as a whole makes it clear that we are to love everyone—husbands must love their wives as Christ loved the church, and so on. Jesus is simply reinforcing the point with strong language so that anyone who chooses to follow him will do so with full commitment. He echoes this call in Luke 9:62 when he declares, "No one who puts a hand to the plow and looks back is fit for service in the kingdom of God."

Theologian, philosopher, and Presbyterian pastor Francis Schaeffer, who is best known for establishing *L'Abri* community in Switzerland, came to faith in Christ as a high school student. When it came time for college, Francis decided to study for the ministry. This decision

---

3. Dietrich Bonhoeffer, *The Cost of Discipleship* (London: SCM Press, 2001), 44.

infuriated his nonreligious father, who told him, "I don't want a son who is a minister."

When the day came for Francis to leave for school, his father objected again. "Dad, I have to go," Francis replied. Enraged, his father slammed the door in his face. Schaeffer later commented that few choices in his life had been more costly than the choice between pleasing the Lord or pleasing his father. His decision led to a fruitful ministry, worldwide influence, and, eventually, his father's salvation.[4]

The Lord also calls his followers to sacrifice themselves, saying, "whoever does not carry their cross and follow me cannot be my disciple" (Luke 14:27). For those who first heard these words, this would have been a particularly dramatic declaration. For a first-century Jew living under Roman domination, people who carried crosses were on their way to execution. The cross did not represent light or momentary hardship; it evoked humiliation, pain, and certain death.

Is Jesus speaking of actual physical death here? Perhaps, for some. However, there is a nuance in the text that points in a different direction. The present tenses Jesus employs in his declaration indicate a continuing process; a more literal translation of his words might be, "Anyone who does not *keep on carrying* his or her cross, who does not keep on following me, cannot be my disciple."

These are strong and difficult words to reconcile, particularly in a society that prizes self-realization as a life goal. Today, many people see the cross as a decoration or an ornament. But Jesus is not calling his followers to wear a necklace—he is calling for full surrender. It has been said that the person who has nothing to die for has nothing to live for. Discipleship is not a casual or an occasional pursuit—we must count the cost.

Following Jesus demands a commitment that transcends our personal relationships, preferences, and resources; Jesus says, "Those of you who do not give up everything you have cannot be my disciples" (Luke 14:33). Notice that the verse says we are to "give up" everything—not "give away" everything. The Lord is not asking us to abandon our families, homes, possessions, or interests. However, he *is* demanding that we give all we have to him. Discipleship entails the daily relinquishing of all we have.

Jesus completes his message by describing the role of disciples in the world: we are to be "salt." This was an idea he had previously introduced

4. Inrig, *The Parables*, 85.

in the Sermon on the Mount, when he said, "You are the salt of the earth. But if the salt loses its saltiness, how can it be made salty again? It is no longer good for anything, except to be thrown out and trampled underfoot" (Matthew 5:13).

Salt was a commodity of great value in the ancient world: it was used in the preservation of food; as a purifying agent; as an antiseptic against destruction or decay; as a seasoning; and as a fertilizer for certain types of plants and soil. There were times when soldiers received their wages (*salary*) in salt. But as Jesus points out, salt that lost its flavor had no use and was simply disposed of.

In 1945, Aleksandr Solzhenitsyn, a Russian dissident, was arrested and spent the next eleven years as a political prisoner. Reflecting on that experience years later, he wrote:

> So what is the answer? How can you stand your ground when you are weak and sensitive to pain, when people you love are still alive, when you are unprepared? What do you need to make you stronger than your interrogator and the whole trap? From the moment you go to prison you must put your cozy past firmly behind you. At the very threshold, you must say to yourself, "My life is over, a little too early to be sure, but there is nothing to be done about it. I shall never return to freedom. I am condemned to die—now or a little later. But later on, in truth, it will be even harder, and so the sooner the better. I no longer have any property whatsoever. For me those I love have died, and for them I have died. From today on, my body is useless and alien to me." Confronted by such a prisoner, the interrogator will tremble. Only the man who has renounced everything can win that victory.[5]

Added to the power of self-renunciation (what you choose to abstain from), the disciple of Christ also has the power to say *yes* to Christ. Saying yes to Jesus, in full surrender, is the pathway to true discipleship.

Dr. Christopher Yuan was a gifted young man who squandered opportunities and blessings. He lived a promiscuous life, began to use drugs, and ended up in prison for dealing them. Soon after he began his sentence, he was diagnosed as HIV positive. Throughout his rebellious years, his parents never quit praying for him. Finally, in his darkest moment in prison, he came to faith.

5. Aleksandr Solzhenitsyn, *The Gulag Archipelago, 1918-1956: An Experiment in Literary Investigation, I–II* (New York: Harper & Row, 1973), 130.

In an address to a large group of university students, Yuan shared his story and ended with the challenge to live with urgency. He said, "The world in which we live today does not need another good Christian—one who simply goes to church every Sunday, but does very little for the kingdom. What this world needs, what this world demands, is not good Christians, but great Christians: Christians who do not settle for mediocrity; Christians who don't follow the ways of the world, but who are fully committed to the ways of Christ."[6]

December 2012 was a life-changing time for a young woman named Kayla Mueller. It was then that she left her home in Prescott, Arizona, hugged her family goodbye and headed to southern Turkey in response to a growing humanitarian crisis. For the next several months, she worked with Syrian refugees who had fled to Turkey in the midst of the Syrian civil war.

On August 3, 2013, Kayla drove to Aleppo in northern Syria with a coworker and friend who was traveling to the Doctors Without Borders hospital for the day. Shortly after her departure from Aleppo, Kayla was abducted by terrorists—the group we have come to know as ISIS.

In July 2014, a U.S. mission to rescue Kayla and others in northern Syria failed. After that, the U.S. lost all track of her whereabouts. However, Kayla was able to smuggle out a letter—a single sheet of paper—with one of the other captives who was released. The letter reads in part as follows:

> . . . if you are receiving this letter it means I am still detained . . . It's hard to know what to say. Please know that I wanted to write you . . . a well thought out letter but . . . I could only write a paragraph at a time, just the thought of you all sends me into a fit of tears . . .
>
> I remember mom always telling me that all in all in the end the only one you really have is God . . . I have come to a place where, in every sense of the word, I have surrendered myself to our creator . . . by God and by your prayers I have felt tenderly cradled in freefall.
>
> I have been shown in darkness, light, and have learned that even in prison, one can be free. I am grateful.
>
> I pray each day that if nothing else, you have felt a certain closeness and surrender to God as well, and have formed a bond of love and support amongst one another . . . I miss you all as if it has been a decade of forced separation.

6. Christopher Yuan, "Centennial" (presentation, Olivet Nazarene University, Bourbonnais, IL, February 22, 2017).

Please be patient, give your pain to God. I know you would want me to remain strong. That is exactly what I am doing. Do not fear for me, continue to pray as will I . . . and by God's will we will be together soon. All my everything . . . Kayla"[7]

On February 6, 2015, ISIS announced that Kayla Mueller had been killed. A few days later, on February 10, her family received official confirmation of her death.

The public knows very little about what this young woman endured during her captivity, but we do know that in the midst of her darkest hour she bore witness that "by God and by your prayers I have felt tenderly cradled in freefall."

Kayla's world had fallen apart. She had fallen into evil hands. Yet, even there, she had the promise of his presence. Her testimony shows that in our darkest hours, rather than giving up or giving in, we can continue to believe in God, to love one another in acts of service and sacrifice, and to bear fruit for the Lord.

## Conclusion

God's word is true every moment of every day of every year. In life's highest places and lowest depths, he will be with you.

In 1519, Hernán Cortés set sail from Santiago, Cuba, with eleven ships, six hundred Spanish sailors and infantry men, and a small number of horses and cannons. He landed on the Yucatán Peninsula, then anchored his ships in the harbor of La Villa Rica de la Vera Cruz. But then Cortés did something that astonished his soldiers: once the cargo of supplies had been offloaded, while they were still on the beach, he ordered that the ships in the harbor be burned to cinders.[8]

Cortés was determined to never turn back. There was no returning to the life they had known; they could now only go forward. This is the type of full commitment Christ demands from those who would follow him.

---

7. "Kayla Mueller: Full Transcript of Letter Sent by US Aid Worker Held Hostage by Isis," *Independent,* last modified February 10, 2015, https://www.independent.co.uk/news/world/middle-east/kayla-mueller-full-transcript-of-letter-sent-by-us-aid-worker-held-hostage-by-isis-10036557.html.

8. Travis Robertson, "'Burn the Ships!'—A Leadership Lesson from Cortés." The Don't Settle Group, Inc., accessed September 2, 2019, https://travisrobertson.com/leadership/burn-ships-succeed-die/.

# 7

# THE PARABLE OF THE TALENTS

Matthew 25:14-30

## The Story *John*

Again, it will be like a man going on a journey, who called his servants and entrusted his wealth to them. To one he gave five bags of gold, to another two bags, and to another one bag, each according to his ability. Then he went on his journey. The man who had received five bags of gold went at once and put his money to work and gained five bags more. So also, the one with two bags of gold gained two more. But the man who had received one bag went off, dug a hole in the ground and hid his master's money.

After a long time the master of those servants returned and settled accounts with them. The man who had received five bags of gold brought the other five. "Master," he said, "you entrusted me with five bags of gold. See, I have gained five more."

His master replied, "Well done, good and faithful servant! You have been faithful with a few things; I will put you in charge of many things. Come and share your master's happiness!"

The man with two bags of gold also came. "Master," he said, "you entrusted me with two bags of gold; see, I have gained two more."

His master replied, "Well done, good and faithful servant! You have been faithful with a few things; I will put you in charge of many things. Come and share your master's happiness!"

Then the man who had received one bag of gold came. "Master," he said, "I knew that you are a hard man, harvesting where you have not sown and gathering where you have not scattered seed. So I was afraid and went out and hid your gold in the ground. See, here is what belongs to you."

His master replied, "You wicked, lazy servant! So you knew that I harvest where I have not sown and gather where I have not scattered seed? Well then, you should have put my money on deposit with the bankers, so that when I returned I would have received it back with interest.

"So take the bag of gold from him and give it to the one who has ten bags. For whoever has will be given more, and they will have an abundance. Whoever does not have, even what they have will be taken from them. And throw that worthless servant outside, into the darkness, where there will be weeping and gnashing of teeth."

—Matthew 25:14–30

## The Window

Before we unpack this story to discover its meaning and application, we should note that Luke records a very similar parable in Luke 19:11–27:

While they were listening to this, he went on to tell them a parable, because he was near Jerusalem and the people thought that the kingdom of God was going to appear at once. He said: "A man of noble birth went to a distant country to have himself appointed king and then to return. So he called ten of his servants and gave them ten minas. 'Put this money to work,' he said, 'until I come back.'

"But his subjects hated him and sent a delegation after him to say, 'We don't want this man to be our king.'

"He was made king, however, and returned home. Then he sent for the servants to whom he had given the money, in order to find out what they had gained with it.

"The first one came and said, 'Sir, your mina has earned ten more.'

"'Well done, my good servant!' his master replied. 'Because you have been trustworthy in a very small matter, take charge of ten cities.'

"The second came and said, 'Sir, your mina has earned five more.'

"His master answered, 'You take charge of five cities.'

"Then another servant came and said, 'Sir, here is your mina; I have kept it laid away in a piece of cloth. I was afraid of you, because you are a hard man. You take out what you did not put in and reap what you did not sow.'

"His master replied, 'I will judge you by your own words, you wicked servant! You knew, did you, that I am a hard man, taking out what I did not put in, and reaping what I did not sow? Why then didn't you put my money on deposit, so that when I came back, I could have collected it with interest?'

"Then he said to those standing by, 'Take his mina away from him and give it to the one who has ten minas.'

"'Sir,' they said, 'he already has ten!'

"He replied, 'I tell you that to everyone who has, more will be given, but as for the one who has nothing, even what they have will be taken away. But those enemies of mine who did not want me to be king over them—bring them here and kill them in front of me.'"

The similarities between the parable in Matthew 25 and this parable in Luke's Gospel are as follows:

- A man goes to another country, stays a long time, then returns.
- The traveler allocates his resources to servants, expecting them to make a profit in his absence.
- The first two servants are faithful; their master then praises them and gives them authority.
- The third servant does not make a profit for his master, but hides what was entrusted to him.
- The third servant tries to justify his actions by accusing his master of being harsh.
- The third servant claims that he was afraid of his master.
- The first two servants are commended and go to heaven; the third is condemned.
- The master tells his unfaithful servant that he should have put the money in the bank.
- The master takes the money he gave the unfaithful servant and gives it to the one who made the most profit.

However, there are also some significant differences between the two stories:

- Jesus tells the two stories at different times in his life.
- In the Luke version, there are ten servants; in Matthew, there are only three.

- In Luke, the master gives each servant the same amount of money (one mina) before he leaves; in Matthew, he distributes the talents according to his servants' ability.
- In Luke, the master instructs the servants to "do business" with the money he's entrusted to them; in Matthew, we see no such statement (though the order to do business seems to be implied).

It is tempting to carry details from the parable over to Matthew's account, or vice versa; but that would be a mistake. These parables, while similar, were told on different occasions, and the differences between them are significant. Yet, even with their differences, it is important to note that both stories emphasize watchfulness and faithfulness: the servants are to eagerly wait and watch for their master's return. As they do so, their master expects them to be faithful stewards of what he's entrusted to them. Jesus ends both stories with similar words: "For whoever has will be given more, and they will have an abundance. Whoever does not have, even what they have will be taken from them" (Matthew 25:29; see also Luke 19:26).

When we review the surrounding context of the Matthew parable, we see that Jesus has been talking with his disciples about the end times and his return. He has also been emphasizing the importance of serving him faithfully while he is gone.

In his classic book, *The Parables of Jesus*, James Montgomery Boice gives five points that are key to understanding the parable of the talents. Those are:

1. There will be a day of future judgment for all people.
2. One aspect of the judgment will be an emphasis on works.
3. All excuses fail before God.
4. The result of the judgment will come as a surprise to many.
5. Jesus speaks of an eternal separation.[1]

In light of these points, the purpose of the parable is to underscore the responsibility that Christ gives to each of his followers. The parable is not about salvation or works righteousness, but about how we use our work to fulfill our earthly callings. It is about the stewardship of every aspect of our lives. The unfaithful steward in this parable didn't

---

1. James Montgomery Boice, *The Parables of Jesus* (Chicago: Moody Press, 1983), 202–207.

just waste the master's money—he wasted an opportunity. As a result, he was judged to be wicked and lazy.

We are responsible for what we do for God with what he has given us, and one day we will be held accountable. The gifts we've received from him—time, talents, influence, resources, health, opportunities—are all given as a sacred trust. They are meant to be used for the Master, and we must be ready to answer for them at any time.

During one of my doctoral programs, I had the privilege of studying with a demanding senior professor named Leon Marsh. He was both feared and respected. He could be harsh and unpredictable—but he was not unfair or unkind. He was simply challenging, for he wanted his students to rise to their full potential. None of his students dared arrive at his class unprepared. During one particular seminar, Dr. Marsh began to feel that we were not doing doctoral-level work. He chastised us and added a major assignment to our workload. One afternoon, about two-thirds of the way through the seminar, we arrived for our usual two-hour session. Dr. Marsh entered the room without a greeting or a smile. He stood silently for a few moments, then said, "Today we are having an exam that will constitute 50 percent of your final grade, along with your seminar paper [which was due at the end of the seminar]. This test will cover everything you have been assigned to this point in the semester."

Dr. Marsh had given us no advance warning of such a major test—we had no idea it was coming. It seemed unfair to spring such an important exam on us with no added time for preparation.

As we sat quietly, Dr. Marsh distributed blue books to each of us and told us we would have one hour to complete the exam. At the end of that hour, we would have to turn in the tests whether we had finished or not. Once again he emphasized that this exam would constitute a major portion of our final grade.

Then, before giving the examination questions, Dr. Marsh said, "Perhaps some of you are unprepared for this exam. I do not want to be unfair, so if any of you would take a grade of C on the test without having to take it, you may do so. Just put your name on the cover of your examination book and leave prior to the exam." We waited for a moment, then two or three students signed their names, gathered their belongings, and left their empty booklets on the desk as they departed. They were happy and relieved to receive a C rather than run the risk of failing the exam.

Once those students were gone, Dr. Marsh reiterated yet again how this test would determine a major part of our grade. He took a set of questions from his briefcase, and just before distributing them said,

"Perhaps some of you are still feeling a bit unprepared for this exam. If you would like to receive a B on the test without having to take it, you may do so. Just put your name on the cover of your examination book and leave prior to the exam."

"So if we leave now, we will get a B on the test?" one student asked.

"Yes, that is correct," replied Dr. Marsh.

There was a flurry of activity as nearly the whole class signed their names and left their tests on the desk as they left. Once they were gone, there were just three of us left—three out of twelve. At that point, Dr. Marsh placed the examination questions back in his case. He smiled for the first time all semester and said, "Okay, y'all got A's. You may sign your names and leave."

That was it. That was the exam. In reality, the only question on the exam (which was never actually asked) was, "Are you ready to give an account of your studies at a moment's notice?"

Over the years, I have forgotten much of what we studied in that class, but I never forgot the primary lesson: be ready.

## The Mirror

Imagine there is a bank that credits your account with $86,400 every morning. Every day, a new deposit goes straight into your account. However, there is one catch: no balance carries over from one day to the next. Every night, the bank removes from your account whatever you failed to use during the day. In that situation, you would withdraw every cent to ensure that nothing was wasted or lost—right?

Every one of us has just such an account—but rather than money, it's filled with time. Every morning, 86,400 seconds are deposited into our accounts. Every night, the account is emptied, and anything that wasn't invested for a good purpose is written off as lost—no balance carries over. The time-bank allows no overdraft.

If you fail to use the day's deposits, the loss is yours. There is no going back; there is no withdrawing against tomorrow. You have to live in the present, on today's deposits. We're all living on borrowed time; make every day count.

In his classic book, *Seven Habits of Highly Effective People*, Stephen Covey writes, "Time management is a misleading concept. You can't really manage time. You can't delay it, speed it up, save it or lose it. No matter what you do time keeps moving forward at the same rate. The challenge is not to manage time, but to manage ourselves."[2]

Scripture uses another word to describe the stewardship of time. Rather than "counting" or "managing" time, the Bible speaks of "redeeming" time—which is an even better idea. Paul writes: "See then that you walk circumspectly, not as fools but as wise, redeeming the time, because the days are evil" (Ephesians 5:15–16, NKJV).

The word "time" in that verse is not the Greek word *chronos*, which denotes clock time—time measured in hours, minutes and seconds. Rather, it is the Greek word *kairos*, which is better translated "the right time" or "the opportune time."

In other words, rather than being called to be good time managers, we are called to be good opportunity managers. It is not just the time, but also timing. Opportunity knocks, but it does not break down the door and drag you off the couch. You must answer.

In the days before modern harbors, a ship had to wait for the tide before it could make it to port. The Latin term for this was *ob portu*, which means waiting "off port"—waiting for *the* moment when the ship could ride the tide to the harbor. The captain and the crew would watch closely for that moment because they knew that if they missed it, the next tide would be a long time coming. It is from the phrase *ob portu* that we get the English word "opportunity."

Life is filled with opportunities. They are God-given interruptions—moments to make your life count. It is for this purpose God gave us speech, hands, feet, strength, and understanding—that we might use them both for our own good and for our neighbor's advantage. Our gifts constitute a calling, a divine vocation to serve the Lord and others with what he's given us. To have a talent is to have a responsibility—but it is also an opportunity.

## Conclusion

The parable of the talents reminds us of our charge: to invest our lives for the kingdom and take care of the King's business until he returns. The parable also warns us against becoming overwhelmed by

---

2. Stephen Covey quoted in Gary Smalley and Ted Cunningham, *Great Parents, Lousy Lovers: Discover How to Enjoy Life with Your Spouse While Raising Your Kids* (Carol Stream, IL: Tyndale House Publishers, Inc., 2010), 60.

fear of failure like the unfaithful servant. Fear is the opposite of faith. When we fear, we lose faith.

But the good news of the parable (as well as the full witness of Scripture) is that our faith, love, and devotion to God can and will cast out fear. Thus the master could say to those who used their talents wisely, "Well done, good and faithful servant! You have been faithful with a few things; I will put you in charge of many things. Come and share your master's happiness!" (Matthew 25:21).

Pastor
Jim
Sharon
John
Kathy
Betty
Jenny
Shirley

# 8

# THE PARABLES OF
# THE HIDDEN TREASURE
# AND PEARL OF GREAT PRICE

Matthew 13:44–46

## The Story  John

The kingdom of heaven is like treasure hidden in a field. When a man found it, he hid it again, and then in his joy went and sold all he had and bought that field.

Again, the kingdom of heaven is like a merchant looking for fine pearls. When he found one of great value, he went away and sold everything he had and bought it.

—Matthew 13:44–46

## The Window  John

These parables occur only in Matthew's Gospel and are part of a series of seven stories grouped in chapter 13. In these stories, Jesus speaks to his disciples about land, fields, seeds, yeast, and weeds—and in the process, paints a beautiful picture of the kingdom of God.

73

Jesus provides interpretations for two of these stories: the parables of the sower and the parable of the weeds. The other five parables that follow are shorter and more pointed. The story of the treasure hidden in a field is contained in a single sentence; the story of the pearl of great price, in just two sentences. They are twins in meaning and in brevity.

Jesus first tells of a man who finds a buried treasure. The man immediately reburies it, then sells all his possessions so he can buy the field and gain the treasure. The parable of the pearl of great price makes a similar point: a merchant, in the course of his trading, finds a single pearl so valuable that he sells all he has to buy it. In both stories, it was the discovery of a lifetime.

Anyone who understands farming knows that land is the essence of a farmer's life. One cannot be a farmer without land; a farmer and his land become one. There is a line from the novel *Gone with the Wind* in which Scarlett O'Hara's father takes her out to the fields and talks about the importance of owning, working, and fighting for one's land. The land, he explains, is "the only thing in this world that lasts."[1]

Yet Jesus presents a story that contradicts this. The most valuable thing in the parable is not the land itself; it's what is hidden in the land that makes it so valuable: "Again, the kingdom of heaven is like treasure hidden in a field, which a man found and hid; and for joy over it he goes and sells all that he has and buys that field" (Matthew 13:44, NKJV). As if the point were not clear enough, Jesus reiterates with a second analogy: "Again, the kingdom of heaven is like a merchant seeking beautiful pearls, who, when he had found one pearl of great price, went and sold all that he had and bought it" (vv. 45–46, NKJV).

The idea of buried treasure may sound antiquated to the modern reader. Today, we have the option to store our wealth in banks, investment companies, safes, lockboxes, even offshore accounts. In Jesus's day, however, burying your riches was a safe and convenient option. But in the event of war, the death of the landowner, or any number of other disasters, the location of buried treasure could be lost forever. In 2014, the *New York Daily News* reported a similar real-life event:

A Northern California couple out walking their dog on their property stumbled across a modern-day bonanza: $10 million in rare, mint-condition gold coins buried in the shadow of an old tree. Nearly all of the 1,427 coins, dating from 1847 to 1894, are in uncirculated, mint

---

1. Margaret Mitchell, *Gone with the Wind* (New York: Pocket Books, 2008), 49.

condition, said David Hall, co-founder of Professional Coin Grading Service of Santa Ana, which recently authenticated them.

Although the face value of the gold pieces only adds up to about $27,000, some of them are so rare that coin experts say they could fetch nearly $1 million apiece. "I don't like to say once-in-a-lifetime for anything, but you don't get an opportunity to handle this kind of material, a treasure like this, ever," said veteran numismatist Don Kagin, who is representing the finders. "It's like they found the pot of gold at the end of the rainbow."

Kagin, whose family has been in the rare-coin business for 81 years, would say little about the couple other than that they are husband and wife, are middle-aged and have lived for several years on the rural property in California's gold country, where the coins were found. They have no idea who put them there, he said. . . .

What makes their find particularly valuable . . . is that almost all of the coins are in near-perfect condition. That means that whoever put them into the ground likely socked them away as soon as they were put into circulation.

Because paper money was illegal in California until the 1870s, he added, it's extremely rare to find any coins from before that of such high quality.[2]

Imagine being one of the people to find this rare, precious treasure. If you had the opportunity to buy the property where it was buried, would you? Of course! And this, Jesus says, is only a glimpse into the infinite value of the kingdom of God. "Sell all," he says, "to buy that field or acquire that one great pearl. The kingdom is worth whatever it takes."

## The Mirror

There are two viewpoints from which to consider these twin parables: the human perspective, and the divine perspective. Both are worthy of consideration.

### *The Human View*

These parables have traditionally been viewed from a human standpoint. The man in the first story and the merchant in the second are seen

2. The Associated Press, "Northern California Couple Find $10M Worth of Rare Gold Coins Buried on Property," *New York Daily News*, February 25, 2014, http://www.nydailynews.com/news/national/northern-california-couple-find-10m-worth-rare-gold-coins-buried-propery-article-1.1701467.

as individuals who, through no effort of their own, have the opportunity to acquire something of great value. Thus, both stories underscore the surpassing value of the kingdom of God—it's worth selling all you have.

These two parables make the spiritual point that the things of this world are worthless compared to the surpassing value of the kingdom of God. Jesus asked, "What good is it for someone to gain the whole world, yet forfeit their soul?" (Mark 8:36). Paul put it like this:

> But whatever were gains to me I now consider loss for the sake of Christ. What is more, I consider everything a loss because of the surpassing worth of knowing Christ Jesus my Lord, for whose sake I have lost all things. I consider them garbage, that I may gain Christ and be found in him, not having a righteousness of my own that comes from the law, but that which is through faith in Christ—the righteousness that comes from God on the basis of faith.
>
> (Philippians 3:7–9)

Notice also that this treasure has to be acquired personally; the two men in the parables could only gain it by giving their all. Many people in Israel would have believed that salvation was a birthright, but these stories underscore the need for a personal decision. In both stories, someone had to "sell all that he had" to buy the treasure of ultimate value—and in real life, that treasure is the kingdom.

This lesson echoes Jesus's words from the Sermon on the Mount: "But seek first his kingdom and his righteousness, and all these things will be given to you as well" (Matthew 6:33). These parables press that point by asking a question: are we willing to sell all that we have to gain the kingdom Jesus describes?

One way he describes it in these parables is as a source of great joy. For both men, the sacrifice of selling all they had was nothing compared to the joy that accompanied the purchase: "in his joy [he] went and sold all he had and bought that field" (Matthew 13:44). R. T. Kendall notes that there are four steps outlined in the parable:

1. You sell all.
2. You surrender all.
3. You sacrifice all.
4. You secure all.[3]

3. Kendall, *The Parables of Jesus*, 66–67.

Until we are willing to part with anything we might value above the kingdom, we can't catch the vision God offers each of us. When we are more interested in accumulating and holding onto money, cars, homes, status, pride—all the modern idols our culture worships—we can neither see nor possess the kingdom of God. Saving faith is characterized by a willingness to surrender all to God; as the hymn "Rock of Ages" says, "In my hand no price I bring; Simply to Thy cross I cling."[4] Salvation comes as we exchange all we are and all we have for Christ. Jesus said, "If anyone desires to come after Me, let him deny himself" (Matthew 16:24a, NKJV).

All of this is true—and yet, there are problems with this interpretation. The human perspective would suggest that people enter the kingdom through their own sacrifice. This contrasts with the teaching that "it is by grace you have been saved, through faith—and this is not from yourselves, it is the gift of God—not by works, so that no one can boast" (Ephesians 2:8–9). Note also that in buying the field and purchasing the pearl, the two men did not actually make a sacrifice, although they sold all they had. As theologian Eta Linnemann writes, "There is a basic difference between a purchase price and a sacrifice. Purchase is directed towards acquiring an object of equivalent value. Sacrifice on the other hand is a giving that expects no reward."[5]

This brings to mind the declaration of Jim Elliot, the missionary martyr who, along with four others, was killed while trying to reach an indigenous tribe with the gospel. After his death, the following quote was found in one of his notebooks: "He is no fool who gives what he cannot keep to gain that which he cannot lose."[6]

### The Divine View

When viewed from a divine perspective, the parables take on a different meaning. In this view, the man in the first story and the merchant in the second represent Christ himself. The field represents the world, as it does in other parables. Thus, the purchases of the field and the pearl

---

4. Augustus Toplady, "Rock of Ages," in *Sing to the Lord*, ed. Ken Bible (Kansas City, MO: Lillenas Publishing Co., 1993), 445.

5. Eta Linnemann, *Parables of Jesus: Introduction and Exposition* (London: SPCK Publishing, 1966), 100.

6. Jim Elliot, *The Journals of Jim Elliot*, ed. Elisabeth Elliot (Grand Rapids: Revell, 1978), 174.

represent Christ's work of salvation on the cross. The treasure represents those who are redeemed by his death and resurrection.

We are the treasure! We are the pearl of great price!

## Conclusion

Should we view these parables from a human or a divine viewpoint? The answer is *both*, because they both help us understand the kingdom of God and our relationship to it. Knowing Jesus as Savior and Lord is more valuable than anything in this world. At the same time, the stories also reveal the great lengths to which God has gone to purchase our salvation. As we read in John 3:16, "For God so loved the world that he gave his one and only Son, that whoever believes in him shall not perish but have eternal life."

*Jerry*
*Shirley*
*John*
*Kathy*
*Rita*
*Betty*

## 9

# THE PARABLE OF THE WISE AND FOOLISH BUILDERS

### Luke 6:46-49

**The Story** *John*

Why do you call me, "Lord, Lord," and do not do what I say? As for everyone who comes to me and hears my words and puts them into practice, I will show you what they are like. They are like a man building a house, who dug down deep and laid the foundation on rock. When a flood came, the torrent struck that house but could not shake it, because it was well built. But the one who hears my words and does not put them into practice is like a man who built a house on the ground without a foundation. The moment the torrent struck that house, it collapsed and its destruction was complete.

—Luke 6:46–49

**The Window** *Bett John*

This parable makes a distinction between hearing and doing. Hearing the sayings of Jesus means that we've cognitively received them so we can understand and remember them. However, *doing* goes much further. Putting the words of Jesus into practice involves the will and the heart. Doing transcends hearing.

The elements of the parable at hand are these: two builders; two houses; two foundations; two storms; and two outcomes.[1]

It sits on two city blocks and rises over one-quarter mile into the sky. It is 110 stories and comprises 4.5 million square feet of office and commercial space. As you drive into Chicago, it breaks the horizon when it is still over twenty miles away. It took two thousand workers working around the clock for nearly three years to build it. And for over twenty years, from its construction in 1973, the Sears Tower stood as the world's tallest building.

The average person might not know all that goes into the engineering and construction of such massive buildings, but one thing is evident: When crews begin to build those great skyscrapers, the first direction they work is not up, but down. Before the building can reach for the sky, it must be anchored on a firm foundation. How true that is of life itself; before you build a life, you must first determine the foundation.

Jesus ended the Sermon on the Mount, the most famous sermon ever preached, with a word about two buildings. One of those buildings stood firm under great stress because it was built on a foundation that enabled it to stand. The other of those two buildings fell suddenly, completely, dramatically, because it didn't rest on a firm foundation.

Jesus calls us to build our lives on a foundation that will last. And that foundation, he says, is a commitment not only to hear, but also to put into practice, as the habit of your life, the Master's words.

## The Mirror

The parable begins with this declaration: "Everyone who hears these words of mine and puts them into practice is like a wise man" (Matthew 7:24). The word "wise" here means prudent. It does not mean genius or exceptional intelligence; you don't have to qualify for Mensa to build a good life. Jesus is not speaking about intelligence, but wisdom. He is saying that if we are prudent and reasonable, we will want to build our lives upon a foundation that lasts.

1. Much of the following material was previously printed in my book *Above All Else* (Kansas City: Beacon Hill Press of Kansas City, 2012), 60–70.

The kind of strong, sudden floods Jesus describes in this passage were not unusual in Israel; in fact, they were expected. Even fools knew to expect such storms during Israel's rainy season. In other words, Jesus is saying that you don't have to be a genius to know your life ought to be grounded on something that can weather the storms that will inevitably come.

In Jesus's parable, this firm foundation is a rock. The term "rock" in Matthew 7:24 does not mean "a detached fragment of stone." This is not a stone that someone might skip, or even a boulder on the ground. Rather, it means rock that is anchored in the depths of the earth—bedrock that cannot be moved. Those floods in Israel are strong enough to carry away huge boulders. This is why Jesus says we should build our lives on bedrock—so we won't be swept away by those powerful storms.

The word "rock" is used differently in different parts of Scripture. For example, when Jesus tells Peter, "On this rock I will build my church" (Matthew 16:18), he uses "rock" to refer to Peter's confession that Jesus is the Christ. 1 Peter 2:6 uses rock language to describe Jesus as the cornerstone; 1 Corinthians 3:10–12 uses it to call Jesus the foundation of the church. But all these uses of "rock" are different than the way Jesus uses it in Matthew 7.

Here, "rock" means "hearing and practicing the Word of God." That is, if you want your life and faith to stand firm, you must go beyond passively hearing the Word of God—you must practice that word in your daily living. You must make God's Word the habit of your life; the inclination of your days; the direction of your walk. We see this in Matthew 7:24: "Therefore everyone who hears these words of mine and *puts them into practice* . . ." (emphasis added). Jesus also reinforces this point in 7:26.

Jesus goes on to emphasize that a firm foundation is fundamental; it is the least visible, but most necessary part of any structure. One of the quickest ways to make your life a disaster is to pile more and more commitments, obligations, and burdens onto a shallow foundation. Your life can only be as large as your foundation can support. That is also true of appearance, the facade, the way life looks.

Most of us are concerned with how we're perceived, and we take great care to look good in public. Many lives are like movie sets—they look great, but they're hollow inside. They're built for the sake of appearance. But Jesus says it's not the appearance of a life that counts—it's the foundation.

The things we fill our lives with are ultimately inconsequential if they do not rest on the foundation of hearing and practicing the Word of God. When life begins to get shaky and the rains descend, we might be tempted to try to fix things by adding to the furnishings. But of course, even the most beautiful furnishings don't matter when the whole house is at risk of collapsing.

If you've ever observed a construction project in progress, you'll also know that foundation work is slow; it takes time to lay a good foundation. You'll notice that in Luke's account of this story, Jesus said a man "dug down deep and laid the foundation on rock" (6:48). There are no quick fixes for a poor foundation.

Several years ago, an office building on the outskirts of London began to develop a series of severe structural cracks. The cracks first appeared on the upper floors of the building. No one seemed too alarmed in the beginning; the cracks were determined to be the result of natural settling that occasionally occurs a few years after a building is completed. However, the cracks grew bigger and began to spread to other floors.

Builders and engineers were summoned to the site, but no one could determine the source of the problem—everything appeared to be in order. Finally, the building architect, who had retired by then, was brought back to the site for consultation. After a careful inspection, he asked to be taken to the basement of the building. He then proceeded down through a series of subbasements that housed some of the mechanical systems.

When he reached the lowest level, he discovered the source of the problem. One large supporting wall in that subbasement had mysteriously been removed. He reported that the cause of the problem had nothing to do with the fourteenth floor, where the cracks had first appeared; the problem was with the foundation.

An investigation was launched, and it was soon determined that an employee who worked in that lower basement had, years before, begun taking a brick or two out of the wall as he left work each day. Over time, he accumulated enough bricks to build a small garage on his property. At first it seemed like no one would ever find out—after all, no one ever came to the subbasement. What the worker did not realize was that, sooner or later, the effects of the weakened foundation would inevitably appear somewhere in the building.

No patching, painting, or propping-up in the world will make up for a faulty foundation. That is true architecturally, but also spiritually. Spiritual reality is not a matter of looking good or feeling good.

It's a matter of coming to grips with the fundamental issues of being Christlike; of hearing his Word and putting it into practice. That is the test of discipleship.

Christ calls us to a life of unwavering obedience. The Christians whose lives will stand and whose faith will respond to the tests of life are those who have reached spiritual bedrock, so that on good days or bad days, joyful days or sad days, their faith still holds steady.

If we could have seen the two houses Jesus describes in the parable, they may very well have looked similar. They were built in the same region, by the same sort of builders, with the same kinds of materials. However, they would only look similar because their foundations weren't visible. The foundation makes all the difference. The same is true of our lives—the important thing isn't what others can see from the outside looking in. Far more important are the things others may not see: the foundation of hearing and practicing the Word of the Lord.

The Santa Monica Mountains overlook Los Angeles. A few years ago, over a period of about nine days, thirteen inches of rain fell on that mountain range. The rain turned the mountainside into mud, and mudslides began making their way toward the beautiful homes perched on stilts along the mountainside. When the mud reached those houses, the stilts gave way, and multimillion-dollar homes tumbled into the valley below as though they were toy houses on toothpicks. One television reporter interviewed a resident as he watched his house slide down the mountainside. When the reporter asked the man what he would do now that his house was gone, the man vowed to rebuild, noting that he had lost two other houses to mudslides in previous years. That seemed foolish—he was paying little attention to the foundation.

The parable of the builders asks us an important question: How are you building? It also implies a second question: Are you ready for the storm?

One house in the parable was built on an outcropping of rock; the other was built on a broad alluvial sand flat that, during the dry season in Judea, may have looked as hard as concrete. But when the rains came, such a place became a floodplain where the waters gathered, roared, and carried away everything in their path. What looks like a foundation—what gives the outward appearance of stability—liquefies so that it can no longer support life.

In the parable, both houses had to face the same, inevitable storm. Likewise, none of us has immunity from life's storms. The question we should be asking ourselves is not, "How can I avoid the storm?" but rather, "How can I prepare to meet and withstand the storm so that when it passes, my life will still be standing?"

This is why storm time is no time to try to fix the foundation. When you are in the emergency room; or you're sitting outside the operating room; or the phone rings in the middle of the night with bad news; you cannot say, "Hold off for a moment while I fix the foundation. Wait while I make some things right." The house of the wise man stood because the builder laid the foundation before the storm ever came.

Jesus said if you hear the Word but fail to practice it in your life; if you think the Word applies to everyone else but you—beware. Your life is built on sand and will surely fall. An unfounded life collapses, but a life founded on God's Word lasts!

### Conclusion

In the end, this parable leaves us with three vital questions:

- How are you building?
- Are you ready for the storms?
- Do you understand the consequences?

Remember, everyone is a builder. Every building will be tested. Only those with a proper foundation will stand. The wise person is the one who not only hears the Word of God but also does the will of the Father. Folly is to hear only and not do.

## 10

# THE PARABLES OF THE WEDDING BANQUET AND GREAT BANQUET

Matthew 22:1–14 and Luke 14:16–24

**The Story** *[handwritten:] John*

Jesus spoke to them again in parables, saying: "The kingdom of heaven is like a king who prepared a wedding banquet for his son. He sent his servants to those who had been invited to the banquet to tell them to come, but they refused to come.

"Then he sent some more servants and said, 'Tell those who have been invited that I have prepared my dinner: My oxen and fattened cattle have been butchered, and everything is ready. Come to the wedding banquet.'

"But they paid no attention and went off—one to his field, another to his business. The rest seized his servants, mistreated them and killed them. The king was enraged. He sent his army and destroyed those murderers and burned their city.

"Then he said to his servants, 'The wedding banquet is ready, but those I invited did not deserve to come. So go to the street corners and invite to the banquet anyone you find.' So the servants went out into the streets and gathered all the people they could find, the bad as well as the good, and the wedding hall was filled with guests.

"But when the king came in to see the guests, he noticed a man there who was not wearing wedding clothes. He asked, 'How did you get in here without wedding clothes, friend?' The man was speechless.

"Then the king told the attendants, 'Tie him hand and foot, and throw him outside, into the darkness, where there will be weeping and gnashing of teeth.'

"For many are invited, but few are chosen."

—Matthew 22:1–14

Jesus replied: "A certain man was preparing a great banquet and invited many guests. At the time of the banquet he sent his servant to tell those who had been invited, 'Come, for everything is now ready.'

"But they all alike began to make excuses. The first said, 'I have just bought a field, and I must go and see it. Please excuse me.'

"Another said, 'I have just bought five yoke of oxen, and I'm on my way to try them out. Please excuse me.'

"Still another said, 'I just got married, so I can't come.'

"The servant came back and reported this to his master. Then the owner of the house became angry and ordered his servant, 'Go out quickly into the streets and alleys of the town and bring in the poor, the crippled, the blind and the lame.'

"'Sir,' the servant said, 'what you ordered has been done, but there is still room.'

"Then the master told his servant, 'Go out to the roads and country lanes and compel them to come in, so that my house will be full. I tell you, not one of those who were invited will get a taste of my banquet.'"

—Luke 14:16–24

## The Window  Shipley

In these passages, Jesus tells the stories of two men who each prepared great banquets and invited many guests well ahead of time. When the time for the banquets arrived, each host sent servants to the invited guests with this message: "Come, for everything is now ready" (Luke 14:17). But in each case, the guests refused to come.

These two parables are very similar and may represent the retelling of the same story on two different occasions, albeit with slightly different emphases. Still, the differences between the Matthew and Luke versions of this parable are noteworthy: In Luke, the story starts with "a certain man;" in Matthew, it is the king. In Luke, it is a "great banquet;" in Matthew, it's a wedding banquet. In Luke, there is one invitation; in

Matthew, there are two. In Luke, the invited guests make excuses; in Matthew, they refuse and turn violent. In Luke, the invited guests are passed by; in Matthew, they are destroyed.

Both versions of this parable are rich with symbolism. We find the Old Testament background for them in Isaiah 25:6–9:

> On this mountain the LORD Almighty will prepare
>     a feast of rich food for all peoples,
> a banquet of aged wine—
>     the best of meats and the finest of wines.
> On this mountain he will destroy
>     the shroud that enfolds all peoples,
> the sheet that covers all nations;
>     he will swallow up death forever.
> The Sovereign LORD will wipe away the tears
>     from all faces;
> he will remove his people's disgrace
>     from all the earth.
> The LORD has spoken.
> In that day they will say,
> "Surely this is our God;
>     we trusted in him, and he saved us.
> This is the LORD, we trusted in him;
>     let us rejoice and be glad in his salvation."

In *Harper's Bible Dictionary,* Paul Achtemeier notes:

"A ritual banquet is one that marks some personal or interpersonal transition or transformation, held to give honor to those undergoing the important social change. As a ritual feature of hospitality, banquets indicate the transformation of a stranger into a guest (Gen. 19:3–14; Luke 5:29) or of an enemy into a covenant partner (Gen. 26:26–31; 2 Sam. 3:20). Banquets mark important transitional points in a person's life, e.g., Isaac's weaning day (Gen. 21:8); the weddings of Jacob (Gen. 29:22), Samson (Judges 14:10), the Lamb (Rev. 19:9), and in the parable of Matthew 22:2–10; the birthdays of Pharaoh (Gen. 40:20), of Herod (Mark 6:21); or the victory banquet hosted by God in Rev. 19:17. At the Last Supper Jesus changes the ceremonial banquet of the Jewish Passover into a ritual banquet effectively symbolizing the meaning of his impending death (Mark 14:12–25 and parallels)."[1]

1. Paul J. Achtemeier, *Harper's Bible Dictionary* (San Francisco: Harper and Row Publishers, Inc., 1985).

The context for the Luke version of the parable is that Jesus is in the house of one of the Pharisee leaders on the Sabbath. While there, Jesus noticed some of the invited guests seeking more honored places to sit. In response, Jesus spoke about humility and seeking the lower position. He then spoke of inviting the poor and the crippled to dinner, even though they could not repay the host, because the host would be repaid in the resurrection.

When giving a dinner, it was customary to invite a certain number of people. Those who accepted the invitation were then counted, and the amount and type of meat to be served would be determined by the number of people who accepted. In those days, once an animal had been killed, it had to be eaten quickly or it would spoil. Therefore, to back out of an invitation at the last minute was particularly rude. The invited guest was duty-bound to attend the banquet.

This makes the first guest's excuse all the more offensive: "I have bought a piece of land and I need to go out and look at it; please consider me excused" (Luke 14:18, NASB). In the Middle East, no one buys a field without first examining it thoroughly. The springs, wells, stone walls, trees, paths, and anticipated rainfall would all be well known long before a discussion of the purchase begins begun. The excuse is therefore invalid and communicates that to the guest, the field is more important than his relationship with the host. In a community where interpersonal relationships are highly important, this excuse is extremely insulting.

Another guest says, "I have bought five yoke of oxen, and I am going to try them out; please consider me excused" (14:19, NASB). Teams of oxen were sold in the Middle East in two ways: First, they could be taken to a marketplace near a field where people could see them plowing a field. Any prospective buyers could then drive the oxen themselves to ensure the animals worked well as a team. Second, the seller could announce that the team was for sale, and a day they would be working the field. On that day, prospective buyers could come to the field to watch the oxen and test them for themselves. Only after the buyer had thoroughly examined the team would a price be discussed. Thus, this guest's excuse is also false and insulting.

A third guest responded, "I have married a wife, and for that reason I cannot come" (14:20, NASB). In tightly knit Middle Eastern communities, weddings were always accompanied by celebrations. The community would have been aware of the wedding and many people would have been invited, with meals prepared beforehand. This man's wedding and the host's banquet would not have been scheduled on the same day.

One by one, the invited guests refuse to partake of the feast that is ready and waiting. What is the host to do? He cannot have a feast without guests. In response, the host invites the unworthy, the poor, the crippled, the blind, and the lame—people who have no way of repaying the host. He is being gracious—very gracious in light of the insults he received.

This parable communicates that no one can enter the kingdom of God without an invitation from him—an invitation by grace. It also is a warning to heed the invitation when you receive it—the invitation will not stand forever. To the original audience of this parable, the invited guests represented the nation Israel, and the poor, lame, etc., represented the gentiles and other outsiders. The host (God) offered the kingdom to Israel, but they rejected the offer. Thus, God gave the kingdom to the gentiles and outcasts who would accept it.

Jesus closes this lesson with a sobering explanation: "many are called, but few are chosen" (Matthew 22:14). Here, the word "many" does not refer to restricted number. In Isaiah 56, the same word is used several times to refer to those for whom Christ poured out his blood. Therefore, the invitation has gone out to all who care to listen. However, some refused; some wanted to come but refused to submit to the requirements for entrance into the kingdom. As many as believed in Jesus—even if they were formerly prostitutes and sinners rather than scholars and sages—would enter the kingdom in the place of these.

## The Mirror

When was the last time you did something for someone who couldn't do anything for you? What are you doing to show the love of Christ to those less fortunate than yourself? Bishop J. C. Ryle wrote, "The Lord Jesus would have us care for our poorer brethren, and help them according to our power. He would have us know that it is a solemn duty never to neglect the poor, but to aid them and relieve them in their time of need."[2] As theologian Philip Ryken explains, "Jesus would have us do this because he wants us to have his heart for people in need—the same heart he had for us when he gave his life for our sins. The guest list he

2. Achtemeier, *Harper's Bible Dictionary.*

gives us—the poor, the crippled, the blind, and the lame—is the guest list of his own grace. These are the very people Jesus came to save."[3]

The parable of the great banquet represents God's gracious invitation to sinners to enter the kingdom of God. As mentioned earlier, the banquet was an ancient symbol of salvation. In the parable of the great banquet, the man hosting the banquet represents God, and the banquet represents his kingdom. God wants to have fellowship with people and satisfy them with good things

The parable in Matthew contains an additional feature that is not included in the Luke version: After his servants have invited "all the people they could find, the bad as well as the good," the king singles out one guest: "But when the king came in to see the guests, he noticed a man there who was not wearing wedding clothes. He asked, 'How did you get in here without wedding clothes, friend?' The man was speechless" (Matthew 22:10–12).

Why is proper dress at a wedding so important? In this passage, the garment represents more than clothing or outward appearance. Revelation 19 states:

> And I heard, as it were, the voice of a great multitude, as the sound of many waters and as the sound of mighty thunderings, saying, "Alleluia! For the Lord God Omnipotent reigns! Let us be glad and rejoice and give Him glory, for the marriage of the Lamb has come, and His wife has made herself ready." And to her it was granted to be arrayed in fine linen, clean and bright, for the fine linen is the righteous acts of the saints.
>
> (Revelation 19:6–8, NKJV)

In this passage, the garment of "fine linen" is defined as "the righteous acts of the saints" (v. 8, NKJV). The Bible uses clothing as an analogy to represent the righteousness Christ imparts to us. Thus, the improperly dressed guest in the parable represents those who seek to join the kingdom without yielding their lives to God.

The king's pronouncement is chilling: "Then the king said to the servants, 'Bind him hand and foot, take him away, and cast him into outer darkness; there will be weeping and gnashing of teeth'" (Matthew 22:13, NKJV). The term "outer darkness" indicates a time of judgment. It is a severe penalty.

3. Achtemeier, *Harper's Bible Dictionary*.

Jesus ends the parable with the declaration that "many are called, but few are chosen" (Matthew 22:14, NKJV). The word "chosen" here applies to those who are not only called, but willingly choose to accept that invitation, being sure to dress in the right garment and remain committed to the kingdom of God.

The king in the parable represents God the Father, and the king's son, of course, is Jesus Christ. In inviting us to the marriage feast, God invites us to prepare now, in this lifetime, for his kingdom, which will be established on the earth when Christ returns.

### Conclusion

Pastor Freddy Fritz tells the following story:

Like most couples preparing for a wedding, Dave Best and his fiancée were probably worried about whether or not everyone would show up on time for the ceremony on July 6, 2008. They didn't need to worry about their friend Dave Barclay, though. He was so excited about the wedding that he showed up a year early!

When Dave Best emailed Dave Barclay, telling him about the July 6 wedding in Wales, Barclay assumed Best meant July 6, 2007. So Barclay bought a plane ticket from Toronto for $1,000. When he landed in Wales, he called Best to get details about the location of the venue for the ceremony. It was only then that Barclay discovered he was a year ahead of schedule.

After a year, Barclay gave it another try. He said, "At least it assured me a mention in the wedding speech!"

We smile at the mistake that this guest made. However, in Jesus's day the problem was not about showing up too early. Jesus constantly warned people about a late arrival or not even bothering to show up at all. The parable of the great banquet illustrates lost opportunity and the amazing grace of God.[4]

---

4. Freddy Fritz, "The Parable of the Great Banquet," Sermon Central, January 30, 2015, https://www.sermoncentral.com/sermons/the-parable-of-the-great-banquet-freddy-fritz-sermon-on-parable-wedding-feast-191194?page=2.

*Pastor*
*Jim*
*Shirley*
*Jerry*
*John*
*Cathy*
*Betty*

*Pastor Retreat*
*Sunday*
*Brownies*
*here*

# 11

# THE PARABLE OF
# THE UNMERCIFUL SERVANT

## Matthew 18:21–35

## The Story *John*

Then Peter came to Jesus and asked, "Lord, how many times shall I forgive my brother or sister who sins against me? Up to seven times?"

Jesus answered, "I tell you, not seven times, but seventy-seven times.

"Therefore, the kingdom of heaven is like a king who wanted to settle accounts with his servants. As he began the settlement, a man who owed him ten thousand bags of gold was brought to him. Since he was not able to pay, the master ordered that he and his wife and his children and all that he had be sold to repay the debt.

"At this the servant fell on his knees before him. 'Be patient with me,' he begged, 'and I will pay back everything.' The servant's master took pity on him, canceled the debt and let him go.

"But when that servant went out, he found one of his fellow servants who owed him a hundred silver coins. He grabbed him and began to choke him. 'Pay back what you owe me!' he demanded.

"His fellow servant fell to his knees and begged him, 'Be patient with me, and I will pay it back.'

"But he refused. Instead, he went off and had the man thrown into prison until he could pay the debt. When the other servants saw what had happened, they were outraged and went and told their master everything that had happened.

"Then the master called the servant in. 'You wicked servant,' he said, 'I canceled all that debt of yours because you begged me to. Shouldn't you have had mercy on your fellow servant just as I had on you?' In anger, his master handed him over to the jailers to be tortured, until he should pay back all he owed.

"This is how my heavenly Father will treat each of you unless you forgive your brother or sister from your heart."

—Matthew 18:21–35

## The Window

Here is a parable that springs directly from a question Peter asks Jesus: "Lord, how many times shall I forgive my brother or sister who sins against me? Up to seven times?" (Matthew 18:21). Perhaps Peter expected Jesus to commend him for his willingness to forgive seven times. Instead, Jesus answered, "I tell you, not seven times, but seventy-seven times" (v. 22).

The parable that follows this exchange is filled with vivid details. First, there is the striking contrast between the two sums of money involved: the servant owed the king ten bags of gold. That was a staggering amount of money—an amount which, in reality, no one could pay, not even the wealthiest men of the day. On the other hand, the debt this man sought to collect from his fellow servant was relatively small by comparison: a hundred silver coins. The stark contrast between such an unpayable debt and such a small amount sets the backdrop for the ensuing drama.

One of the unforgiving servant's faults was that he demanded more of others than he was prepared to do himself—he preferred the silver coins to the golden rule. This is an all-too-common mistake: judging others at their worst and ourselves at our best. Moreover, it's the exact opposite of the behavior Jesus demands: treat others as you would have them treat you.

The parable serves as a reminder of the colossal and unpayable debt we owe to God. It also reminds us that any wrong that's been done to us is of little consequence compared to the wrong we've done him. As C. S. Lewis declared, "To be a Christian means to forgive the inexcusable because God has forgiven the inexcusable in you."[1] The story also demonstrates the magnitude of God's forgiveness—his mercy is infinite.

---

1. C. S. Lewis, *The Weight of Glory* (New York: Harper Collins, 2001), 181.

One lesson of the parable is the link between the forgiveness we've received from God and the forgiveness we extend to others. This memorable story demonstrates the contrast between God's mercy and the human response, which too often emphasizes law above love.

This principle was introduced in the Sermon on the Mount, where Jesus told his disciples, "Blessed are the merciful, for they will be shown mercy," and, "forgive us our debts, as we also have forgiven our debtors" (Matthew 5:7, 6:12). Knowing about forgiveness and being forgiving are two different matters. Again, C. S. Lewis put it well: "Every one says forgiveness is a lovely idea, until they have something to forgive."[2]

There is a story of a man who was bitten by a dog that was later discovered to have rabies. By this time, the man was desperately ill, and medical science had not yet developed a treatment for the disease.

The doctor broke the news to the man: "Sir, we will do all we can do to make you comfortable, but I will not give you false hope. Your condition is terminal. There is nothing we can do. My best advice is that you put your affairs in order as soon as possible."

The man sank back in the bed in shock. But later that day, he asked for a pen and paper. When the doctor returned to the room, he said, "I am so pleased that you are writing out your will and last wishes."

"I am doing nothing of the kind," the man retorted. "I am making a list of all the people I want to bite before I die!"

Many people live and die with such a list: a list written in their minds and hearts, if not on paper, of those who have mistreated them. Sometimes, there are not specific names—just a deep sense of bitterness that life has been unfair.

## The Mirror

The gospel's call is to be forgiven and forgiving. Forgiveness is at the heart of the kingdom's economy: It saves the expense of anger, the cost of hatred, and the waste of joy. S. I. McMillen observed in his book, *None of These Diseases*, "The moment I start hating a man, I become his slave. He even controls my thoughts. I can't escape his tyrannical grasp on my mind."[3]

Forgiveness does not mean that the offense never happened or that it did not matter. Forgiveness does not erase the past; it enlarges the

2. C. S. Lewis, *Mere Christianity* (New York: HarperOne, 2001), 115.
3. Inrig, *The Parables*, 73.

future. It helps the one who has been hurt to be set free from carrying the burden. Forgiveness isn't earned; it has to be granted. It sets the stage for new beginnings.

It's been said that when it comes to forgiveness, there are four different types of character: First, people who are easily provoked and easily pacified—their loss is easily placated by what they gain in return. Second, people who are hard to provoke, but also hard to pacify; their gain continues to be overshadowed by their loss. Third, people who are hard to provoke and easy to pacify; these are good people. Fourth, people who are easy to provoke and hard to pacify. It is to that fourth type of person that Jesus directs this parable.

There are three important truths that flow from this story: First, the source of our forgiveness is God's forgiveness.

Second, our refusal to forgive is costly. To accept God's forgiveness and refuse to forgive others is wicked. That might seem harsh, but the king's words are, "you wicked servant" (Matthew 18:32). The unforgiving servant grabbing his debtor around the neck to choke him is a startling picture. An unforgiving spirit can choke the life out of a marriage, a family, a friendship, or a work relationship.

Third, the secret of forgiveness is grace. Receiving grace means we must express grace: "Be kind and compassionate to one another, forgiving each other, just as in Christ God forgave you" (Ephesians 4:32). Forgiveness is evidence that we have become new creatures in Christ, and that the Spirit of Christ lives within us.

In Johan Bojer's novel *The Great Hunger*, the protagonist is a man named Peer Holm. Holm lives beside a neighbor who owns a vicious dog. After nearly being attacked by the dog, Holm threatens to call the sheriff. The neighbor curses Peer Holm and refuses to control the dog.

A few days later, Holm is working when he hears screams. He runs and sees his neighbor's dog attacking his young daughter. Holm tears the dog away from her, but it's too late—his little girl is gone.

The sheriff shoots the dog, and the villagers want to run the neighbor out of town. They ostracize him from the community and refuse to speak or deal with him. The boys in the village hoot at him and throw rocks at him. When spring arrives, the neighbor plows and prepares his field, but no one will sell him any seed. His field lies fallow.

Then, one early morning, Peer Holm can no longer take it. He gets up, takes some of his own grain, and quietly sows it in his neighbor's field.

Why would a grieving father extend such kindness to his mortal enemy? In Peer Holm's words, he does it so "that God might exist" in their community.[4]

There is power in forgiveness.

Corrie ten Boom and her sister, Betsie, were imprisoned in a German concentration camp at Ravenswood during World War II. One specific guard was particularly harsh. Years later, during a meeting held in post-war Germany, ten Boom bore witness to the grace of God that had sustained her through her suffering. After her talk, as she was visiting with those who had attended the meeting, ten Boom suddenly saw the guard who had been so cruel to her. He was there in the room. He had heard her speak.

A rush of pain and anguish rose within her as she recalled all she had suffered at that prison guard's hands. Cautiously, humbly, the man approached ten Boom, and through his tears, asked if she would forgive him. In that moment, the pain of the past gave way to the mercy and grace she had received—and the guard who did not deserve it received her forgiveness and blessing.

Jesus concludes the parable with these words: "This is how my heavenly Father will treat each of you unless you forgive your brother or sister from your heart" (Matthew 18:35). James echoes this later in the New Testament when he writes, "For judgment is without mercy to one who has shown no mercy. Mercy triumphs over judgment" (2:13, ESV).

The purpose of forgiveness is twofold. First, it is to show grace in light of the grace we have received. Second, it is to show gratitude in light of what God has done for us. Forgiveness not only releases an offender from a debt they may owe—it also frees the one who has been offended from carrying the weight of that offense. Both people are freed. It's as Shakespeare wrote in *The Merchant of Venice*: "The quality of mercy is not strain'd / It droppeth as the gentle rain from heaven / Upon the place beneath: it is twice blest; / It blesseth him that gives, and him that takes."[5]

When forgiveness flows through us, we become conduits of God's forgiveness. Thomas Edward (T. E.) Lawrence was born on August 16, 1888, in Wales. Popularly known as Lawrence of Arabia, Lawrence became famous for his exploits as British military liaison to the Arab Revolt during World War I. The desert raids of Lawrence and his Arab

4. Johan Bojer, *The Great Hunger* (New York: The Century Co., 1919), 324.
5. William Shakespeare, *The Merchant of Venice*, act 4, sc. 1.

rebels distracted many Turkish troops who could have been fighting the main British forces in the Middle East. Lawrence of Arabia's struggle against the Turks during World War I is a legendary example of guerrilla warfare, and his personal account, *The Seven Pillars of Wisdom,* has become a classic of world literature.

During the war, Lawrence formed close friendships with many Arabian sheikhs. After the war, he brought some of these sheikhs back to England to show his appreciation for their support against the Turkish forces. They had a wonderful visit, appeared before the House of Commons and Parliament, and had an audience with the queen.

On the last night of the sheikhs' visit, Lawrence offered them anything they wanted to take back with them to their desert homes. The sheikhs led him up to the hotel room, into the bathroom, and pointed to the faucets in the bathtub. They said they wanted to take faucets with them so they could have running water in the deserts. The sheikhs did not realize that the faucets were superficial: Behind them was plumbing, a water heater, an energy source that heated the water, a city main that supplied the water, and from the city main, a line to an outside source of water. The magic was not in the faucet—it was what was behind the faucet.

This is a reminder of how God gives us the grace for forgiveness. That grace does not flow from us, but through us. Forgiveness is the only way to come to terms with a world filled with hurt, disappointment, and injustice. Forgiveness is love's toughest work. It's an unnatural act, for it stands in contrast to our sense of fairness—our sense that people should pay for the wrong they have done. While it is true that nothing can change the past, forgiveness can change the future.

**Conclusion**

In his classic book *Forgive and Forget: Healing the Hurts We Don't Deserve,* Dr. Lewis B. Smedes writes that forgiveness unfolds through four stages:

> The first stage is *hurt:* when somebody causes you pain so deep and unfair that you cannot forget it, you are pushed into the first stage of the crisis of forgiving.
>
> The second stage is *hate:* you cannot shake the memory of how much you were hurt, and you cannot wish your enemy well. You sometimes want the person who hurt you to suffer as you are suffering.

The third stage is *healing*: you are given the "magic eyes" to see the person who hurt you in a new light. Your memory is healed, you turn back the flow of pain and are free again.

The fourth stage is the *coming together*: you invite the person who hurt you back into your life; if he or she comes honestly, love can move you both toward a new and healed relationship. The fourth stage depends on the person you forgive as much as it depends on you; sometimes he doesn't come back and you have to be healed alone.[6]

Forgiveness does not mean that the hurt or wrong did not happen or that it doesn't matter. Forgiveness does not excuse or minimize what was done. Again, forgiveness isn't natural. It's supernatural—God-given. That doesn't mean that it's automatic or that it happens in a moment. Generally, forgiveness is a process—often a painful process. It happens in bits and pieces, in starts and stops and setbacks—yet it is possible and it is worth it. As Smedes writes, "We are never so free as when we reach back into our past and forgive a person who has caused us pain."[7]

Genuine forgiveness must be rooted in realism—a firm facing of the facts. However, it does not dwell there. The grace of forgiveness looks forward, in light of the past; yet it does not let that light color the path to the future. Forgiveness is love's answer to hate. It is an open and honest release within the mind, heart, and will of the one who has been injured. It results in a new vision and a new feeling as hope replaces hate.

How often shall we forgive? Seven times? No. Jesus said, "I tell you, not seven times, but seventy-seven times" (Matthew 18:22).

6. Lewis B. Smedes, *Forgive and Forget: Healing the Hurts We Don't Deserve* (San Francisco: Harper & Row, 1984), 2.

7. Smedes, *Forgive and Forget*, 114.

*Pastor*
*Jim*
*John*
*Kathy*
*Karen*
*David*
*Betty*
*Shirley*
*Jerry*

## 12

# THE PARABLE OF THE LOST SHEEP

Matthew 18:12–14 and Luke 15:3–7

## The Story *John*

What do you think? If a man owns a hundred sheep, and one of them wanders away, will he not leave the ninety-nine on the hills and go to look for the one that wandered off? And if he finds it, truly I tell you, he is happier about that one sheep than about the ninety-nine that did not wander off. In the same way your Father in heaven is not willing that any of these little ones should perish.

—Matthew 18:12–14

Then Jesus told them this parable: "Suppose one of you has a hundred sheep and loses one of them. Does he not leave the ninety-nine in the open country and go after the lost sheep until he finds it? And when he finds it, he joyfully puts it on his shoulders and goes home. Then he calls his friends and neighbors together and says, 'Rejoice with me; I have found my lost sheep.' I tell you that in the same way there is more rejoicing in heaven over one sinner who repents than over ninety-nine righteous persons who do not need to repent."

—Luke 15:3–7

101

The Window ) | メ٦

This is among Jesus's simplest and most familiar parables—but its familiarity does not dull its appeal. The closer we look at this story, the more we see.

To those who first heard it, the story of a shepherd and his flock would have been familiar. There were sheep on nearly every hillside. Jesus's original audience also understood the close relationship between a shepherd and his sheep—the sheep know their shepherd's voice.

In both the Matthew and Luke accounts of the parable, Jesus begins by asking a question. In Matthew he asks, "If a man owns a hundred sheep, and one of them wanders away, will he not leave the ninety-nine on the hills and go to look for the one that wandered off?" (18:12). In Luke's version, Jesus personalizes the question: "Suppose one of you has a hundred sheep and loses one of them. Does he not leave the ninety-nine in the open country and go after the lost sheep until he finds it?" (Luke 15:4).

Generally speaking, sheep are social animals and naturally group together. If one wanders off, it can easily become bewildered and often will lie down and simply wait to be found. Shepherds could often number their flock with an extended glance, but in addition to that intuitive reckoning, they would generally count the sheep in the morning, noontime, and just before sunset.

When he notices that one of the flock is missing, a good shepherd will leave the flock and set off to find the lost sheep. Once he found it, the shepherd would often carry the sheep across his shoulders so he could make better time getting back to the flock. The image is tender and comforting.

Jesus adds another element to this simple story: Once he found the lost sheep, the shepherd calls his friends and neighbors saying, "Rejoice with me; I have found my lost sheep" (Luke 15:6). Jesus reveals the parable's meaning with a word of commentary: "I tell you that in the same way there is more rejoicing in heaven over one sinner who repents than over ninety-nine righteous persons who do not need to repent" (15:7).

Thus, the parable of the lost sheep illustrates Christ's attitude toward the lost: He seeks them, finds them, and carries them to safety. Scripture says, "We all, like sheep, have gone astray, each of us has turned to our own way; and the LORD has laid on him the iniquity of us all" (Isaiah 53:6). What a portrait of God! The good shepherd is one of the Bible's most poignant allegories.

This story reveals much about God's love:

1. The love of God is an *individual* love. He knows each one and cares for his children individually. The fact that ninety-nine percent of the sheep are safe does not change the shepherd's concern for the one that is missing.
2. The love of God is a *seeking* love. The shepherd is not content to wait for the lost sheep to return—he goes looking for it. This brings to mind Jesus's statement about himself in Luke 19:10: "For the Son of Man came to seek and to save the lost." The shepherd feels personally responsible for each sheep.
3. The love of God is a *protecting* love. The shepherd willingly sets out to find the lost sheep and protect it from the dangers of being alone. In John 10:11–18, Jesus calls himself the good shepherd who not only searches for lost sheep but also lays down his life for them.
4. The love of God is a *rejoicing* love. When the shepherd finds the lost sheep, he joyfully lifts it onto his shoulders and goes home. Afterward, he calls his friends and neighbors together and says, "Rejoice with me; I have found my lost sheep." The inconvenience, the miles, the dangers and darkness the shepherd endured, all fade at the moment the sheep is found.

Luke is careful to note the context of this story: Jesus was surrounded by tax collectors and "sinners" who had come to listen to him. The Pharisees and teachers of the law took offense at the presence of these people, muttering, "This man welcomes sinners and eats with them" (Luke 15:2). Let that accusation sink in for a moment. When you hear those words, rejoice! You—in fact, all of us—are included in that category. If Jesus did not welcome sinners, he would not have welcomed you or me.

It was in this setting, as he was being criticized for keeping company with sinners, that Jesus told the story of the lost sheep. In that setting, with the Pharisees leaning in to listen, the flock represented them—the religious Jews. The lost sheep represented those who had wandered off and separated themselves from the rest—the tax collectors and sinners. Jesus's point was that those who had wandered away were still precious enough for the Shepherd to seek and find.

Shirley

## The Mirror

Throughout history, artists have depicted the parable of the lost sheep in many ways. One of the most familiar is a painting by Alfred Soord that depicts a shepherd perched precariously on a high ridge, holding onto a rock above him with one hand while reaching down to a stranded sheep on the ledge below. Another compelling detail is the presence of vultures already circling, waiting to tear into their helpless prey should the shepherd fail.[1]

Luke arranges this parable as the first of a trio: the lost sheep, the lost coin, and the lost son, all found in Luke 15. The portraits of a seeking shepherd, a weeping woman, and a waiting father reinforce the image of a God who seeks and finds.

The poet Francis Thompson was born in northwest England in 1859. When he was eighteen, his parents enrolled him at Owens College, Manchester, to follow in his father's footsteps and study medicine. However, Thompson was restless and soon left college for London, hoping to pursue a career as a writer. What followed was a downward spiral of a once-promising life: He fell into despair, became addicted to opium, and found himself sleeping on the banks of the Thames with London's homeless. He sold matches just to stay alive.

Yet it was during this time, in the midst of all his hunger, deprivation, homelessness, and hopelessness, that Thompson was most able to see the kingdom of heaven and sense God's pursuing love. In the midst of his devastating experiences, he began to hone his poetic focus and insights. In 1888, Thompson sent a tattered and torn manuscript to the periodical *Merry England*. Its editors, Wilfrid and Alice Meynell, devout Christians themselves, not only recognized Thompson's poetic ability, but took him under their care and gave him a home. They also arranged for the publication of his first book in 1893, simply titled *Poems*, which included his masterpiece, "The Hound of Heaven," which reads in part:

> I fled Him, down the nights and down the days;
> I fled Him, down the arches of the years;
> I fled Him, down the labyrinthine ways
> Of my own mind; and in the mist of tears
> I hid from Him, and under running laughter.
> Up vistaed hopes I sped;

1. Alfred Soord, *The Lost Sheep*, 1900, Church of St. Barnabas, London.

And shot, precipitated,
Adown Titanic glooms of chasmèd fears,
From those strong Feet that followed, followed after.
But with unhurrying chase,
And unperturbèd pace,
Deliberate speed, majestic instancy,
They beat—and a Voice beat
More instant than the Feet—
'All things betray thee, who betrayest Me.'

As the poem unfolds, Thompson paints a portrait of the God who continues to follow the one who has "fled him." In the last stanza, the seeking God finally finds the one who is lost:

Halts by me that footfall:
Is my gloom, after all,
Shade of His hand, outstretched caressingly?
'Ah, fondest, blindest, weakest,
I am He Whom thou seekest!'[2]

That declaration by God—"I am He Whom thou seekest"—is what Jesus portrays in the story of the lost sheep. As God declared through the prophet Ezekiel, "I will search for the lost and bring back the strays" (34:16).

## Conclusion

The story of the lost-then-found stray is our story. God does more than passively wait for his wandering children to return—he pursues them and rejoices when they are found. We find in the parable a portrait of the God who rejoices whenever the lost are found; the broken are healed; the alienated are reconciled; the sick are made well; the oppressed are freed; the prisoner is released; the humble are lifted up; and the dead are brought back to life.

2. Francis Thompson, "The Hound of Heaven," *The Poems of Francis Thompson*, ed. Brigid M. Boardman (New York: Continuum, 2001), 35.

*Pastor*
*Jerry*
*Shirley*
*John*
*Kathy*
*Jim*
*Betty*

## 13

# THE PARABLE OF THE RICH FOOL

Luke 12:15–21

## The Story *John*

Then he said to them, "Watch out! Be on your guard against all kinds of greed; life does not consist in an abundance of possessions."

And he told them this parable: "The ground of a certain rich man yielded an abundant harvest. He thought to himself, 'What shall I do? I have no place to store my crops.'

"Then he said, 'This is what I'll do. I will tear down my barns and build bigger ones, and there I will store my surplus grain. And I'll say to myself, "You have plenty of grain laid up for many years. Take life easy; eat, drink and be merry."'

"But God said to him, 'You fool! This very night your life will be demanded from you. Then who will get what you have prepared for yourself?'

"This is how it will be with whoever stores up things for themselves but is not rich toward God."

—Luke 12:15–21

## The Window

In Luke 12:13, a listener in the crowd surrounding Jesus asks him to tell his brother to equitably divide the inheritance due to him. Jesus declines, then uses the occasion to teach his disciples that a godly life is more important than material things. To illustrate this, he tells a parable. This story tells of a man who enjoyed a run of unbroken prosperity. He was wealthy at the beginning of this story, but a surprising harvest makes him even more so—he is so prosperous that his barns cannot hold all his produce. His biggest problem seems to be what to do with his abundance. His solution is to tear down his old barns and build bigger ones, then sit back and enjoy himself in the years to come. However, in doing so, he becomes the victim of his own abundance. His thinking, values, plans, and purposes rest on the wealth he's accumulated, and soon, his possessions possess him. Just when it seems he has it all, death comes calling.

There is a real gravity to greed. It weighs us down and pulls us away from life's higher pursuits. In this way, greed is the enemy of our own well-being. It is like drinking saltwater; it only increases our thirst. It blinds us to the fact that "we brought nothing into the world, and we can take nothing out of it" (1 Timothy 6:7).

Alexander the Great, realizing he could not take any of his possessions or honors with him when he died, asked that upon his death, his body be positioned in the coffin to show that his hands were empty. The conqueror of the world knew that he could not take his conquests or the spoils of those battles with him.

Although it might seem grim at first, one of St. Benedict's rules was "To have the vision of death before one's eyes daily."[1] The goal of the rule was not a preoccupation with death, but a motivation to seize each day as a glorious gift.

Jesus cautions in his Sermon on the Mount, "Do not store up for yourselves treasures on earth, where moths and vermin destroy, and where thieves break in and steal. But store up for yourselves treasures in heaven, where moths and vermin do not destroy, and where thieves do not break in and steal. For where your treasure is, there your heart will be also" (Matthew 6:19–21).

There's the story of a rich young man who was driving his Rolls-Royce on a mountain road when he lost control and his car plunged

1. St. Benedict, *The Rule of St. Benedict,* trans. Cardinal Gasquet (New York: Dover Publications, Inc., 2012), 9.

over a cliff. The young man was thrown clear of the vehicle, but his left arm was severed in the process. He stumbled to his feet and stood at the top of the cliff, looking down at the burning wreck of his car.

"My Rolls! My Rolls!" he cried.

The driver of another car stopped to help and heard him crying out. He gently grabbed the man and said, "Sir! You are in shock. Your arm has been severed! Let me help you. "

The young man looked down, and when he saw that his arm was gone he cried, "My Rolex! My Rolex!" Greed can make us blind to what is truly important in life.

The parable of the rich fool does not condemn prosperity. However, it does underscore two miscalculations on the farmer's part. First, he assumed that because he had done well, he would continue to do well, and his fortunes would increase. His second error was assuming that he could live in the future off the profits of the past. He believed that his earnings belonged to him solely for his pleasure and ease.

In response, God tells him, "You fool! This very night your life will be demanded from you. Then who will get what you have prepared for yourself?" (Luke 12:20). In the Bible, the term "fool" refers to a person who does not acknowledge the existence of God. The farmer was rich in the world's eyes and in his own eyes, but when life ends—what then?

Material things are designed for this life, not for the life to come. Therefore, the man in the story invested all his life, time, and talents for this life, but failed to plan for the life to come. His hope and confidence was in his possessions. He didn't realize that life and all we "own" is only ours on loan. The farmer, as a result, became a hollow person—barns full, but life empty. The man was rich, yet all he had died with him. Jesus sums up the parable with this concluding statement: "This is how it will be with whoever stores up things for themselves but is not rich toward God" (Luke 12:21).

Peter Gomes, the longtime pastor of Memorial Church on the Harvard University campus, observed, "The one who is rich toward God, Jesus says, is the one who recognizes here and now that treasure is not in what one has, or even in what one leaves or gives away . . . Those are not riches. Treasure is in who one is, and ultimately that treasure is defined in terms of the relationship one has with God."[2] Those who would truly be rich and secure in their future are those whose treasure is in heaven.

2. Peter Gomes, *Sermons: Biblical Wisdom for Daily Wisdom* (New York: Avon Books, 1998), 67.

## The Mirror

The parable of the rich fool is certainly a stern warning against greed, but it is more than that. It is also a portrait of an inauthentic existence—an existence which, in the end, is empty. The story calls to mind the words of David Brooks, the esteemed *New York Times* columnist and commentator, who reflected on living life for your eulogy rather than your résumé:

> I've been thinking about the difference between the résumé virtues and the eulogy virtues. The résumé virtues are the ones you put on your résumé, which are the skills you bring to the marketplace. The eulogy virtues are the ones that get mentioned in the eulogy, which are deeper: Who are you? Are you bold, loving, dependable, consistent?
>
> Most of us would say that the eulogy virtues are the more important of the virtues. But at least in my case, are they the ones that I think about the most? The answer is no.
>
> So I've been thinking about that problem, and an individual who has helped me think about it is a guy named Joseph Soloveitchik, who was a rabbi who wrote a book called *The Lonely Man of Faith*.
>
> He said there are two sides of our natures, which he called Adam I and Adam II. Adam I is the ambitious, external side of our nature. He wants to build, create, create companies, create innovation. Adam II is the humble side of our nature. Adam II wants not only to do good, but to be good, to live in a way internally that honors God and our possibilities.
>
> Adam I wants to conquer the world. Adam II wants to hear a calling and obey. Adam I savors accomplishment. Adam II savors inner consistency and strength. Adam I asks how things work. Adam II asks why we're here.[3]

In his story, "How Much Land Does a Man Need?," Leo Tolstoy writes about the Russian peasant who is told that he can have all the land he can walk around in the time between sunup and sundown. So, with the rising of the sun, the peasant begins walking as fast as he can. By midmorning, it seems that he's moving too slowly. So he increases his pace and doesn't stop for lunch.

As the afternoon heat beats down on him, he hurries his pace even more. He feels that he must circle more and more land. By late afternoon,

---

3. David Brooks, "Should You Live for Your Résumé . . . or Your Eulogy?" Filmed March 2014 in Vancouver, BC. TED video, 3:20. https://www.ted.com/talks/david_brooks_should_you_live_for_your_resume_or_your_eulogy/transcript.

he's soaked with sweat from head to toe. He is exhausted. He had walked around a huge section of land, but still he yearns for more. So, he begins to run. Breathlessly, he pushes himself into a deeper fatigue than any he had ever known. His heart beats wildly. Sundown is only a few minutes away, so he runs faster. But as he races toward his beginning point, the point that would make him the largest landholder in the district, his heart gives out and he falls to the ground dead.[4]

This story reminds me of the old cliché about the man who loses his health trying to accumulate wealth, and then loses his wealth trying to regain his health. Proverbs 23:4 warns against this foolish philosophy when it says, "Do not wear yourself out to get rich; do not trust your own cleverness." Proverbs 11:4 adds, "Your riches won't help you on Judgment day; only righteousness counts then" (TLB).

## Conclusion

The parable finds its turning point and climax in God's declaration: "This very night your life will be demanded from you" (Luke 12:20). However, the parable is not just about the irony of dying at the peak of self-indulgence. Rather, the story is about what the man's passing reveals: the folly of living simply for "more." More is never enough.

Therefore, the point of the parable of the rich fool is twofold: First, we are not to devote our lives to accumulating wealth. The parable makes an interesting point when God says to the farmer, "And the things you have prepared, whose will they be?" This echoes the expression of Ecclesiastes 2:18: "I hated all my toil in which I toil under the sun, seeing that I must leave it to the man who will come after me" (ESV).

There was nothing wrong with the farmer's desire to build more barns; that desire was both wise and prudent. The problem is that he had no thought of sharing. In the original Greek, the personal pronoun "my" occurs four times in this parable, and "I" occurs eight times. Even in the English we see that "my" occurs four times and "I" appears five times. Notice the farmer's language: *my* crops, *my* barns, *my* goods. He confused stewardship with ownership; he forgot that

4. Leo Tolstoy, "How Much Land Does a Man Need?" (Houston: Calypso Editions, 2010).

all he had belonged to God. So it is with us. What we have is not ours to own; it is ours on loan.

The second point of the parable of the rich fool is that God does not bless us so we can hoard our wealth to ourselves. We are blessed to be a blessing in the lives of others, and we are blessed to build the kingdom of God. The Bible says if our riches increase, we must not set our hearts upon them (Psalm 62:10).

One morning in 1888, the inventor of dynamite, Alfred Nobel, was forced to face the question of his life's true value when he read his own obituary in a French newspaper. Obviously, it was a journalistic mistake. One of his brothers had died, and a careless reporter had used a prewritten obituary of the wrong man. But as he read, Nobel was shocked and deeply disturbed to learn what the world really thought of him. He was seen as the dynamite king, the merchant of death, who had amassed a great fortune out of explosives.

Nobel had hoped his inventions would be useful to the world; but instead, he was portrayed as a man who dealt in blood and war for profit. At that moment, Alfred Nobel resolved to show the world the true purpose of his life. He revised his will so that his fortune would be dedicated to the recognition of great creative achievements, with the highest award going to those who had accomplished the most for world peace. From then on, Nobel's image began to change. Now, more than a century later, we remember him the way he wanted to be remembered—we all associate him with the Nobel Peace Prize.

In Luke 12:21, we find the theme and the summary of this parable. "So is he who lays up treasure for himself, and is not rich toward God" (NKJV). Jesus is not saying that Christians should be poor but that we must watch our attitude toward money and the things of this world. As Matthew 6:21 says, "Where your treasure is, there you heart will be also."

If we allow money and the material things of this world to dominate our thoughts and the focus of our lives, we end up idolizing those things, and our hearts will be geared toward the pursuit of those things. The famous warning in 1 Timothy 6:10—"For the love of money is a root of all kinds of evil"—makes it clear that it is the *love* of money that is "a root of all kinds of evil," not the money itself.

Having money is not a problem—but our attitude toward it can become a problem. We need to regard our finances as a tool that we steward for the Lord. Rather than becoming possessive of our money and letting the world dictate what we spend it on, let us instead allow

God to lead us in how to use our resources—after all, they are ultimately his anyway.

In contrast to the foolishness of the farmer, the last three words of the parable—"rich toward God"—indicate where true wisdom lies. We are to be rich in the things of God—toward the things that will last. Here's how to do that:

1. Don't be arrogant.
2. Don't trust in money.
3. Enjoy life without being selfish.
4. Be rich in good works.
5. Be generous.[5]

First Timothy 6:19 says, "In this way they will lay up treasure for themselves as a firm foundation for the coming age, so that they may take hold of the life that is truly life."

5. Kendall, *Parables*, 181.

14

# THE PARABLE OF THE
# RICH MAN AND LAZARUS

## Luke 16:19–31

## The Story

There was a rich man who was dressed in purple and fine linen and lived in luxury every day. At his gate lay a beggar named Lazarus, covered with sores and longing to eat what fell from the rich man's table. Even the dogs came and licked his sores.

The time came when the beggar died and the angels carried him to Abraham's side. The rich man also died and was buried. In Hades, where he was in torment, he looked up and saw Abraham far away, with Lazarus by his side. So he called to him, "Father Abraham, have pity on me and send Lazarus to dip the tip of his finger in water and cool my tongue, because I am in agony in this fire."

But Abraham replied, "Son, remember that in your lifetime you received your good things, while Lazarus received bad things, but now he is comforted here and you are in agony. And besides all this, between us and you a great chasm has been set in place, so that those who want to go from here to you cannot, nor can anyone cross over from there to us."

He answered, "Then I beg you, father, send Lazarus to my family, for I have five brothers. Let him warn them, so that they will not also come to this place of torment."

Abraham replied, "They have Moses and the Prophets; let them listen to them."

"No, father Abraham," he said, "but if someone from the dead goes to them, they will repent."

He said to him, "If they do not listen to Moses and the Prophets, they will not be convinced even if someone rises from the dead."

—Luke 16:19–31

## The Window ) *Jerry*

Of this parable, James Montgomery Boice wrote: "In all the Bible I do not believe there is a story more stirring or more disturbing than that of the rich man and Lazarus. It is stirring for its description of two men, one rich and one poor. They are set in contrast, and the contrast is not only between their circumstances in life but also between their circumstances to come."[1]

Of all the parables, this is the only one in which any of the characters is given a proper name. The two main characters are the rich man and the beggar. Tradition has given the name *Dives* (which is Latin for "rich") to the rich man, but that name does not appear in the story. The beggar is named Lazarus, which is the Greek form of the Hebrew name Eleazar, which means, "God is my help." Perhaps the beggar is given this name to underscore that God helps even the poorest and most vulnerable among us.

As the story unfolds, there are many details that emphasize the rich man's wealth and luxury. His clothing is described as "purple and fine linen"—the first-century equivalents of silk sheets and designer clothing (Luke 16:19). The story notes that he "lived in luxury every day" (v. 19). His lifestyle was sumptuous; he enjoyed lavish surroundings, rich food, and self-indulgent habits daily.

In contrast, Lazarus lives in desperate poverty at the rich man's gate. The beggar is described in the most pitiful terms—sores cover his body, and he is laid (thrown) at the gate daily, longing for the crumbs from the rich man's table. It is a dramatic contrast; the two men live at the opposite poles of affluence and misery. However, there is a deeper contrast between the two—one that has nothing to do with economic status, is invisible to the human eye, and is revealed only after death.

1. James Montgomery Boice, *The Parables of Jesus* (Chicago: The Moody Bible Institute, 1983), 210.

This dramatic picture sets the stage for the second set of contrasts, which we see after the men's deaths. Lazarus's death probably came as a surprise to no one and was mourned by few. What follows in the parable, however, would have surprised most of Jesus's original audience. It was widely believed that misery on earth was the result of sin or some sort of divine disapproval. Yet Lazarus, instead of enduring more torment after he died, was favored by God; Jesus declared, "the angels carried him to Abraham's side" (v. 22).

"Abraham's bosom," as some translations render it, was a phrase used to describe the highest bliss of paradise. To be in Abraham's bosom was to be in a place of special intimacy, fellowship, and care. In his Gospel, John loves to describe himself as "the one who had leaned back against Jesus at the supper" (21:20). Lazarus's position at Abraham's side conveys a clear picture of his exultation to a place of honor. Death transformed him from an outcast at the gate to an honored guest at the head table.

The rich man also dies. One can only imagine the expensive and elaborate funeral of such a wealthy man. In death, as in life, his body would have been well cared for; yet, in his case, dying as he lived also meant that he made no provision for his soul. Neither money nor luxury could follow him past the grave. No angels carried him to Abraham's side. Instead, the wealthy man found himself in a place of constant torment.

In life, Lazarus longed for a crust of bread from the rich man's table, but now, in death, the wealthy man begs for a single drop of water. This reversal of fortunes raises a question: Why? Why did Lazarus go to Abraham's side, while the rich man found himself in hell?

Perhaps the deeper message of the parable is revealed in the dialogue between the rich man and Abraham. Once the rich man sees the beggar in heaven, he calls out:

> "Father Abraham, have pity on me and send Lazarus to dip the tip of his finger in water and cool my tongue, because I am in agony in this fire."
> But Abraham replied, "Son, remember that in your lifetime you received your good things, while Lazarus received bad things, but now he is comforted here and you are in agony. And besides all this, between us and you a great chasm has been set in place, so that those who want to go from here to you cannot, nor can anyone cross over from there to us."
>
> (Luke 16:24–26)

Having been denied even temporary relief from his pain, the rich man makes one more request: "Then I beg you, father, send Lazarus to my family, for I have five brothers. Let him warn them, so that they will not also come to this place of torment" (16:27–28). The rich man realizes that his brothers are also headed for torment unless they change their ways—they need to be warned so they will repent.

Abraham does not entertain the rich man's request, however: "They have Moses and the Prophets; let them listen to them. . . . If they do not listen to Moses and the Prophets, they will not be convinced even if someone rises from the dead" (16:29, 31). Skeptics may resist it, but God's Word is clear, sufficient, and powerful. People who are not changed by Scripture or the witness of godly men and women will not be changed by a miracle. Thus, the rich man finds himself in torment because he has not listened to God's Word.

The tormented man's appeal also reveals something beyond concern for his family: implicit in his request is an attack on God himself. The rich man is suggesting that he did not have a fair chance; that God did not make the stakes clear enough; that if God would have sent someone from the dead to him, he would have believed. Thus, his torment is really God's fault!

Saying, "I will believe if only God will make it clear enough. If I don't believe, that's God's fault," is a very twentieth-century idea. On one occasion, someone asked the eminent British philosopher and Nobel Prize winner Bertrand Russell, author of the book *A History of Western Philosophy* and the essay "Why I Am Not a Christian," what he would say if he found himself before God on judgment day and God said to him, "Why didn't you believe in me?"

In response, Russell shot back, "I will tell him he just did not give me enough evidence."[2]

This attitude refuses to see that God speaks and has spoken to all of us through creation, through history, in his Word, and through his Son. Yet people still demand a sign.

## The Mirror

As we gaze into this story, the reflection we see raises several important issues.

First, this parable forces us to think seriously about death and the life to come. In an interview about his life and work, the filmmaker Woody Allen was asked, "Aren't you happy that you will achieve a measure of

2. Ravi Zacharias, *Can Man Live Without God?* (Nashville: Word Publishing, 1994), 182.

immortality through your achievements?" Allen replied, "Who cares about achieving immortality through achievements? I am interested in achieving immortality through not dying!"[3]

There is no immortality that does not involve the end of life as we now know it. Rich or poor, we will all die and face our eternal destinies. Our present relationship with God determines our eternal relationship with him.

The parable also addresses the potential consequences of abundance. Prosperity can often be deceiving. As educational philosopher Robert Maynard Hutchins said, "Our real problems are concealed from us by our current remarkable prosperity, which results in part from our new ways of getting rich, which is to buy things from one another that we do not want, at prices we cannot pay, on terms we cannot meet, because of advertising we do not believe."[4]

Finally, another major theme in the parable is responsibility. The rich man's desire for his family to be saved from eternal torment suggests that when it comes to caring for people's eternal souls, our time is limited; if we want to help others spiritually, we must do so while we are still living. Our responsibility for the poor is also at the heart of the story. We must not leave them at our gate. The gospel compels us to reach out to the needy and help them in every way we can.

## Conclusion

A few years ago, a collection of artifacts from the grave of the ancient pharaoh Tutankhamun was exhibited in Chicago at the Museum of Natural History. It was amazing to see all of the treasure and artifacts that were placed in King Tut's tomb.

I have been to Cairo and Upper Egypt, stood in the Valley of the Kings outside of Luxor, and viewed the site of King Tut's tomb. It was all very impressive. However, there is another tomb in Egypt that, for me, is even more noteworthy. It is the grave of a young American named William Borden.

By the time Bill Borden graduated from a Chicago high school as heir to the Borden Dairy fortune, he was already a millionaire. For his

3. Inrig, *The Parables*, 121.
4. Robert Maynard Hutchins quoted in Donald McCullough, *Waking from the American Dream: Growing Through Your Disappointments* (Downers Grove, IL: InterVarsity Press, 1988), 73.

high-school graduation present, his parents gave him a trip around the world. He then attended Yale University. During his college years, Borden made an entry in his journal that defined who he was going to be and what he was going to do with his life. That entry said simply, "Say 'no' to self and 'yes' to Jesus every time."

From Yale, Borden went on to Princeton Seminary to prepare for a life of missionary service. When he finished his studies at Princeton, Borden left America for the mission field. Because he was hoping to work with Muslims, he first stopped in Egypt to study Arabic. However, shortly after his arrival, he contracted spinal meningitis, and within a month, twenty-five-year-old William Borden was dead. Like young King Tut, his life was cut short.

Borden was buried in Egypt, but his Bible was sent home, along with his other belongings. In the flyleaf of his Bible he had written these words: "No reserves," "No retreats," and "No regrets."

Not many people go to see Bill Borden's grave in Egypt. No museums display his belongings. Nevertheless, his life had meaning—for just as he had received Christ Jesus as Lord, he continued to live his life "in Christ."

*Pastor Jim*
*Kathy-John*
*Betty Jerry-Shirley*

## 15

# THE PARABLES OF THE MUSTARD SEED AND THE YEAST

### The Story    *John*

He told them another parable: "The kingdom of heaven is like a mustard seed, which a man took and planted in his field. Though it is the smallest of all seeds, yet when it grows, it is the largest of garden plants and becomes a tree, so that the birds come and perch in its branches.

He told them still another parable: "The kingdom of heaven is like yeast that a woman took and mixed into about sixty pounds of flour until it worked all through the dough."

—Matthew 13:31–33

Again he said, "What shall we say the kingdom of God is like, or what parable shall we use to describe it? It is like a mustard seed, which is the smallest of all seeds on earth. Yet when planted, it grows and becomes the largest of all garden plants, with such big branches that the birds can perch in its shade."

—Mark 4:30–32

121

Then Jesus asked, "What is the kingdom of God like? What shall I compare it to? It is like a mustard seed, which a man took and planted in his garden. It grew and became a tree, and the birds perched in its branches."

Again he asked, "What shall I compare the kingdom of God to? It is like yeast that a woman took and mixed into about sixty pounds of flour until it worked all through the dough."

—Luke 13:18–21

## The Window

The parable of the mustard seed appears in all three of the Synoptic Gospels. Jesus uses this analogy to describe the growth of the kingdom of God: It begins small, but develops into a powerful force that meets the needs of all who seek refuge in it. Jesus was fond of using the mustard seed as an illustration; besides this parable, he used it when his disciples could not cast out a demon from a child: "Truly I tell you, if you have faith as small as a mustard seed, you can say to this mountain, 'Move from here to there,' and it will move. Nothing will be impossible for you" (Matthew 17:20). On another occasion, Jesus used the same idea of "mustard-seed faith" to describe complete forgiveness:

"If [your brothers or sisters] sin against you seven times in a day and seven times come back to you saying 'I repent,' you must forgive them."

The apostles said to the Lord, "Increase our faith!"

He replied, "If you have faith as small as a mustard seed, you can say to this mulberry tree, 'Be uprooted and planted in the sea,' and it will obey you."

(Luke 17:4–6)

In this instance, Jesus introduced the parable of the mustard seed by saying, "What shall we say the kingdom of God is like, or what parable should we use to describe it? (Mark 4:30). In the Matthew and Luke accounts, this brief story is immediately followed by the parable of the yeast, which shares the theme of the kingdom of heaven growing from small beginnings: "He told them still another parable: 'The kingdom of heaven is like yeast that a woman took and mixed into about sixty pounds of flour until it worked all through the dough'" (Matthew 13:33).

In both of these stories, Jesus paints a hopeful picture of the growth of the kingdom. In the parable of the soils, only a portion of the seed falls on good soil and produces a harvest. In the parable of the wheat and weeds, the weeds in the field hinder the growth of the kingdom. Yet, in spite of those obstacles, Jesus tells these stories to assure his followers of the kingdom's ultimate triumph.

As Jesus says in the parable, mustard seeds are very tiny—smaller than the head of a pin. Even hundreds of them can cover only a small part of your palm. They are indeed the least of the seeds. Once they sprout, however, the plants can grow to be ten to twelve feet high and provide shelter and support for birds that perch on their limbs—quite a large output from such a small beginning.

Yeast is a spore that permeates a lump of dough and causes it to expand and soften. The spore is even smaller than a mustard seed—virtually invisible. Yet it is capable of filling, multiplying, then expanding a ball of dough to several times its original size. These parables illustrate the kingdom's small beginnings.

Just how small did the kingdom begin? Consider the circumstances of Jesus's birth. The accounts in the Gospels portray a very humble beginning. Born into a young family from Nazareth, Jesus was delivered in Bethlehem, the smallest of villages. The circumstances of his birth were meager; it was quite a small start for the King of Kings.

Jesus's ministry also started small, and in the smallest of places—Galilee was a backwater region of an obscure part of the Roman world. Christ ventured no farther than Jerusalem with his message.

In the Roman Empire's perspective, Jerusalem was not considered a cultural center; Rome, Athens, and Alexandria featured more prominently on the political and cultural radar of that world. To the Romans, Jerusalem was a city of fanatics and seditious Jews best kept in check by legions of troops and pliant vassal kings like Herod.

Jesus taught about the kingdom of God from the beginning of his ministry; Mark 1:15 records Jesus entering Galilee, saying, "The time is fulfilled, and the kingdom of God is at hand. Repent, and believe in the gospel" (NKJV). Though many thousands of people were impacted by Jesus's message, by the end of his life, only a few more than a hundred disciples endured (see Acts 1:15). The church indeed grew, but compared with the general population, it remained quite small. Nevertheless, the seed of the kingdom was planted. It began very small, then grew in stages.

Mark's Gospel prefaces the parable of the mustard seed with another parable from Jesus:

The kingdom of God is as if a man should scatter seed on the ground, and should sleep by night and rise by day, and the seed should sprout and grow, he himself does not know how. For the earth yields crops by itself: first the blade, then the head, after that the full grain in the head. But when the grain ripens, immediately he puts in the sickle, because the harvest has come.

(Mark 4:26–29)

Pastor David Strain tells of the death of one of his parishioners, Joseph Leake. Leake died at ninety, and according to his daughters, he lived and died like a pauper. He watched television, but not on his own set—he watched the neighbor's television in their home to avoid the cost of buying his own set. He delayed repairs on his home for as long as he could; he shopped at Goodwill and other thrift stores and wore second-hand clothing. He was, to all observers, a poor old man.

However, when he died, Leake left an estate of just over two million dollars—all of it hard-earned and carefully saved throughout his long and frugal life. The remarkable thing about Joseph Leake was that no one—not even his friends or family—knew about his wealth. Appearances, it turns out, can be deceiving.[1]

In a way, that is precisely Jesus's point about the kingdom of heaven: Appearances can be deceiving. What may at first seem inadequate, small, or insignificant means for reaching the world will in the end prove to be mighty, expansive, and potent as God works out his purposes and advances his kingdom against all odds.

But the truth is that "the kingdom of heaven is like a mustard seed." Easily overlooked, often dismissed—that's the nature of the kingdom. "God chose what is low and despised in the world, even things that are not, to bring to nothing things that are" (1 Corinthians 1:28, ESV). God takes his Son and hangs him on the cross; he is despised and rejected. Yet that very seed plants the kingdom in the world.

The parables speak not only of an improbable growth, but also an invisible power—like yeast, which pervades the entire loaf. That is what the kingdom is like: we cannot see it working; it is mysterious in its progress. However, its potency is nonetheless irresistible. The parable

---

1. David Strain, "The Parables of the Mustard Seed and the Leaven," April 6, 2014, https://www.fpcjackson.org/resource-library/sermons/the-parables-of-the-mustard-seed-and-the-leaven.

of the mustard seed emphasizes the kingdom's extensive growth; the parable of the yeast emphasizes its intensive power.

The Jews of Jesus's day were expecting a messiah who would overthrow the Romans and establish a mighty kingdom on earth; these parables were designed to paint a different picture. Jesus redefines the coming of the kingdom: it was not like the mighty cedars of Lebanon; it was, at first, a tiny, hidden presence on earth. Yet, over time, it would develop into a mighty tree.

Jesus's life mirrors this truth. He was not born in a palace or a stately home, but in a tiny town on the outskirts of the Roman Empire. He was raised in a carpenter's home. He became a rabbi without credentials or standing among the religious leaders of his day. His earthly life ended on a cross—and yet, in that moment, a seed was sown that would yield a mighty kingdom.

## The Mirror

The mustard seed and the yeast also illustrate the kingdom coming in an individual way, in our own lives. The mustard seed implies that it is not great faith he requires of us, but faith in a great Savior. The *object* of our faith is the key, and God wants to grow your faith in him into something far greater than you could have imagined.

Søren Kierkegaard noted that life has to be lived forward but can only be understood backward. It is often only when we look back across the landscape of our lives that we see God's plan unfolding.

I enrolled as a college student at the university where I now serve as president when I was eighteen. I started as a business major with plans to return to Ohio to work with my father, who was developing his own newspaper and publishing business. After my sophomore year, however, I felt a call to ministry. I assumed that meant I would be a pastor—that was the only concept of ministry I had at the time.

So, late in the summer, before returning to college for my junior year, I told my father that I felt called to ministry. He said to me, "You're already halfway through your business degree. Maybe you should finish that degree and then, if you still feel the same way when you graduate, you could go on to seminary for your ministerial training." He was confident that my business training would be helpful even if I did go into ministry.

That was reasonable advice—good advice—but I did not take it. I felt that I had to say yes to my call to ministry rather than defer my decision to a later time. Therefore, at the beginning of my junior year, I changed my major from business to religion and set my sights on an unknown future.

A few weeks after that conversation with my father, the editor of the school yearbook asked if I would be in a photo for the yearbook. I agreed, and when I showed up on campus to have the picture taken, I found I would be posing with three other people: a female student selected at random; the student council president; and the president of the university, Dr. Harold Reed.

Whenever I look back at that photo, I can't help but marvel at God's providence. On the right side of the photo is Dr. Reed, who would go on to become the longest-serving president in the university's history. On the left side of the frame, only a few feet away, is a student (me) who would also become the same university's president and, by God's grace, surpass Dr. Reed's record of service. Who knew?

However, the best part of that picture is that the girl standing beside me, Jill, is now my wife. We were friends but had never had a date. However, within a few weeks of that photo being taken, I asked her out—and the rest is history. Or maybe I should say "*His* Story," for I have come to believe that photo was providential.

Just a few weeks before the photo, I had said no to a publishing career with my father, who went on to establish a successful business (when my dad retired, he owned nine newspapers and had a large commercial printing business). Though I didn't realize it on the day that photo was taken, God had something better—something much better for me and for Jill.

Isn't that just like our heavenly Father—he who is "able to do exceedingly abundantly above all that we ask or think" (Ephesians 3:20, NKJV); he who declared, "I know the plans I have for you . . . plans to prosper you and not to harm you, plans to give you hope and a future" (Jeremiah 29:11)? That photo captured not only what was—two students, chosen at random, standing with the university president—but also what was yet to come.

## Conclusion

The parables affirm that grace is like a mustard seed or a bit of yeast sown in us; it transforms us and sets God's plans and purposes in motion. The kingdom continues to come on earth as it is in heaven—but it often comes in unexpected ways.

Years ago, in a little out-of-the-way town in Ohio, a young man and his wife were just getting started in life and beginning to raise a a little girl and little boy. The parents were good people, but they did not know Christ. Their children were growing up without the influence of the church.

The husband had been raised in a wonderful Christian family, and his father was a Presbyterian pastor. On one occasion, his mother, a godly woman, came to Ohio for a visit. She stayed several days, and during that time, she realized that her son and his family were not going to church. In response, she began to pray.

One morning, just before she left to go home, the grandmother walked to the end of the street. As she walked, she prayed. She prayed that somehow the Lord would find a way to reach her family. At the end of the block, she noticed a man working out in his yard. He greeted her with a friendly smile, so she stopped for a moment to talk. During their conversation, she sensed that this person might be an answer to her prayers.

"Do you go to church?" she gently asked the man.

"Oh, yes," he replied. "I'm the Sunday school superintendent at the Church of the Nazarene here in town."

The grandmother didn't know much about the Church of the Nazarene, but she could tell that this was a good man. So she told him that she was visiting her family and asked, "Would it be possible for you and your wife to pay a visit to my son and his family? And perhaps you could find a way for the children to get to Sunday school?"

"I would be happy to do that," he replied.

A few days after the grandmother left, the man—Earl Granger was his name—walked to the other end of the block and knocked on the door. When the lady of the house answered, he introduced himself and told her that he was from the Church of the Nazarene. "Would it be possible for me and my wife, Clelah, to stop by on Sunday to take the kids to Sunday school?"

The mother hadn't been raised in church and didn't have any real interest in it. However, the thought of an hour or so of quiet on Sunday morning was appealing.

"That would be fine," she replied. "I'll have them ready."

So beginning the next Sunday, Earl and Clelah Granger began taking those children to Sunday school and church. After a few weeks, it was time for vacation Bible school. The children begged to go, and the parents agreed. Those were the days when vacation Bible school lasted a full week and culminated in a big program on Sunday where children would recite the verses they had learned, sing the songs they had been singing all week, and display their crafts.

All the parents of the children were invited. Somewhat reluctantly, this mom and dad agreed to go. When they arrived, they received a warm greeting and recognized some other young couples from town. And of course, they were very proud of their children.

The following week, the pastor paid them a visit and invited them to come to church again. They were not sure whether they wanted to, but they were open to the idea. They did return a time or two during the next month or so—and soon, they came to faith. This was a couple who, when they went in, they went *all* in. They quickly became fully engaged in the life of that little Nazarene church.

A few months later, the father, who worked as a truck driver, was driving in the dead of winter and got into a snowstorm. He decided to pull off the road and let the storm pass. As he pulled into the next town, he began to look for a place to park his truck for the night.

As he rounded a gentle bend, he saw a neon sign through the snow. At first, he thought the sign might belong to a motel or restaurant where he could wait out the storm. As he got a little closer and as the snow cleared a bit, he read the sign: "Olivet Nazarene College."

He didn't think much about it and drove a little farther to a place where he could park. The next day was bitterly cold, but the snow had stopped. As he headed back out of town, he came around the bend and saw the sign again, next to a large, stately-looking limestone building.

"Olivet Nazarene College," he thought. "I'm a Nazarene. I wonder if my children could ever come to a school like this."

The years passed; his children grew. Sure enough, when it was time for college, his children—first his daughter, then, a year or so later, his son—went to that school. And, thirty years ago, on the evening I was installed as the president, I had dinner in the president's home with that man, his wife, and their daughter, Jill, who is now my wife. The saintly grandmother's prayers and the Sunday school superintendent's faithfulness not only changed the life of that young couple—they also changed Jill's life, and mine too.

"Then Jesus asked, "What is the kingdom of God like? What shall I compare it to? It is like a mustard seed, which a man took and planted in his garden. It grew and became a tree, and the birds perched in its branches.""

## 16

# THE PARABLE OF THE PHARISEE AND THE TAX COLLECTOR

Luke 18:9–14

### The Story

To some who were confident of their own righteousness and looked down on everyone else, Jesus told this parable: "Two men went up to the temple to pray, one a Pharisee and the other a tax collector. The Pharisee stood by himself and prayed: 'God, I thank you that I am not like other people—robbers, evildoers, adulterers—or even like this tax collector. I fast twice a week and give a tenth of all I get.'

"But the tax collector stood at a distance. He would not even look up to heaven, but beat his breast and said, 'God, have mercy on me, a sinner.'

"I tell you that this man, rather than the other, went home justified before God. For all those who exalt themselves will be humbled, and those who humble themselves will be exalted."

—Luke 18:9–14

### The Window

The parable of the Pharisee and the tax collector reveals two different ways of approaching God, as demonstrated in the stark contrast between the two men and their prayers. The first character in the story is a Pharisee, a devout religious leader. Jesus's listeners would not have been surprised to hear Jesus talk about a Pharisee going to the temple for prayer—that's what everyone expected of Pharisees.

However, they would have been startled to hear about a tax collector doing the same. The tax collectors were collaborators with the Roman Empire, and most people thought they had no regard for God. Therefore, there is tension in this story right from the start.

The contrast between the two men is apparent in both the posture and content of their prayers. The Pharisee enters the temple filled with a sense of self-righteousness. He opens his prayer by addressing God—or so it seems. However, a closer examination suggests that he is really talking to himself.

The English Standard Version of the Bible translates the beginning of verse 11 as follows: "The Pharisee, standing by himself, prayed thus." However, the New King James Version's translation is also valid: "The Pharisee stood and prayed thus with himself." That translation might better capture what is happening in this scene: Outwardly, the Pharisee was addressing God, but really, he was talking "with himself" aloud so that others could hear him.

It is also noteworthy that the Pharisee does not confess his sins to God; nowhere in his prayer does he ask God to forgive him for what he has done to violate God's law. In fact, he seems too preoccupied with his virtues to acknowledge his need for God. He declares, "God, I thank you that I am not like other people" (v. 11b). He then specifies the other people he's referring to: "extortioners, unjust, adulterers, or even like this tax collector" (v. 11c, ESV). Clearly, the Pharisee compares himself with other people. However, he does not compare himself with holy and godly people; instead, he compares himself with the sorts of people who are infamously sinful.

The Pharisee then commends his good works to God: "I fast twice a week; I give tithes of all that I get" (v. 12, ESV). Darrell Bock summarizes the Pharisee's prayer thus: "In effect his prayer is, 'I thank you, God, that I am such a great guy!' Pride permeates the intercession."[1]

Pastor Martin Collins notes:

1. Darrell Bock, quoted by Freddy Fritz, "Grace Alone," Sermon Central, October 5, 2017, https://www.sermoncentral.com/sermons/grace-alone-freddy-fritz-sermon-on-grace-225169?page=3&wc=800.

The Pharisee glories in what he is ("I am not like other men"), what he does ("I fast twice a week"), and what he gives ("I give tithes of all that I possess"). Self is a prominent feature of his prayer—he uses the personal pronoun "I" five times—showing his great obsession with himself. He does not pray for others, and frankly, he has no interest in them other than to point out their faults. Not satisfied with commending himself, he disdains the tax collector as well, when he should have interceded for him before God. His prayer shows that he thinks of God as being impressed with pettiness and severity.[2]

The Pharisee approaches God based on his own righteousness—his own works and good deeds—and believes that God will accept him because of it. Moreover, he looks down on those who are less righteous. It is very dangerous when "self" occupies the center of someone's life—an all-too-common problem. Luke notes that some of the people Jesus addressed in this passage trusted in their own righteousness and treated others with contempt.

The tax collector's prayer was much different than the Pharisee's, beginning with his posture: "But the tax collector, standing far off, would not even lift up his eyes to heaven, but beat his breast, saying. . ." (v. 13, ESV). Unlike the Pharisee, the tax collector doesn't even lift his eyes to heaven—he is so remorseful for his sins that he stands with downcast eyes and beats his breast in shame, praying, "God, be merciful to me, a sinner!" (v. 13, ESV).

We see here that the tax collector does not compare himself to anyone else; he knows he is a sinner who deserves God's wrath and judgment. He does not ask God for justice. Instead, he begs him for mercy.

Another noteworthy element of the tax collector's prayer is his spirit of confession. His prayer is simple, humble, and direct as he pleads, "God, have mercy on me, a sinner" (18:13). Confession is a necessary element for all who come to God in prayer: We must confess our devotion to God, our need for his grace, and our desire for Christ to be Lord of our lives.

Of the tax collector's humble and sincere prayer, Jesus says, "I tell you, this man went down to his house justified" (v. 14, ESV). The word "justified" in this text is a legal term that means being declared "not guilty."

2. Martin G. Collins, "Parable of the Pharisee and the Tax Collector," Church of the Great God, December 2004, http://www.cgg.org/index.cfm/fuseaction/Library.sr/CT/BS/k/1000/The-Parable-of-Pharisee-and-Tax-Collector.htm.

Jesus's commentary indicates that this story is not primarily a parable about prayer, but about salvation. The prayers reveal two different approaches to God. The Pharisee bases his confidence on his good works. He hopes and expects to be justified by his performance.

The tax collector, on the other hand, approaches God with humility, recognizing both his sin and God's mercy—his only hope. His prayer is one of the shortest in all the Bible: seven words in the English translation, and only six words in the original Greek. It is short yet sincere, brief but bold in its plea for mercy.

## The Mirror

In 2013, the *Oxford English Dictionary* chose "selfie" as its word of the year. With the advent of mobile phones with built-in cameras, the "selfie" phenomenon has become ubiquitous. Facebook, Instagram, Snapchat, and other platforms have provided myriad avenues for documenting the details of our daily life in photographs. In the process, social media has fostered a self-focus that can easily creep into our thinking about God. Too many have fashioned God in their own image rather than seeking to conform to his.

Pastor David Roseberry notes that if social media had existed in Jesus's time, this parable might have taken a slightly different form:

> A Pharisee went to pray in the temple. He knelt down, took out his phone, and adjusted his robes so he looked perfectly powerful. He was about to tweet a pic of his pious self, but then he saw another guy—a tax collector!—bending low to the ground across the sparsely crowded room. The Pharisee sneaked a quick pic of himself with the now prostrate tax collector in the background. Tap, tap, tap on the brightly lit screen, and off to the cloud it went. His tweet hit his few hundred followers moments later: #Praying here next to a tax collector! #GoodLuck #NoChance #Loser #ThankingGodI'mNotLikeHim! #Blessed #PhariseePride.[3]

The culture around us certainly fosters an inflated sense of self-importance: "Who *wouldn't* want to see me at Disney World, or know where I'm having lunch, or what I just bought at the mall?" This self-interest is inherent to us as fallen beings. We seem to be hard-wired

3. David Roseberry, *Giving Up: How Giving to God Renews Hearts, Changes Minds, and Empowers Ministry* (Franklin, TN: New Vantage Books, 2017), 38–39.

to ask: What's in this for me? How does this make me look? How will this make me feel?

This parable cautions us that until Christ fundamentally re-centers and re-orients us, our lives will be warped by self-focus, out-of-balance with him and who he has created us to be. It also reminds us that we can be religious without being godly or righteous. As Martin Luther warned, "Our nature has been so deeply curved in upon itself because of the viciousness of original sin that it not only turns the finest gifts of God in upon itself and enjoys them . . . indeed, it even uses God himself to achieve these aims, but it also seems to be ignorant of this very fact."[4]

It's easy to worship God's gifts without worshiping God. In a selfie theology, God becomes our benefactor; he exists to meet our needs and watch over us, rather than for us to glorify him. Too easily, we adopt a consumerist attitude toward worship. When that happens, our focus centers not on God, but on ourselves—what music we like; what message we want to hear; what groups we want to attend. It's tempting for pastors and congregations alike to start thinking that if they want their church to grow, they have to focus on the congregation rather than God.

The tax collector exhibits precisely the sort of attitude Jesus spoke about in the Sermon on the Mount: "Blessed are the poor in spirit, for theirs is the kingdom of heaven" (Matthew 5:3). Being poor in spirit means admitting that we have nothing to offer God to atone for our sins. The tax collector recognizes his sinful condition and seeks the only thing that can bridge the gap between himself and God—he prays, "Have mercy on me" (Luke 18:13).

## Conclusion

The Bible often warns us to avoid pride. Notice what Solomon writes about how God views pride: "The fear of the LORD is to hate evil; pride and arrogance and the evil way and the perverse mouth I hate" (Proverbs 8:13, NKJV). However, God gives grace to those who humble themselves; the apostle James wrote, "But He gives more grace. Therefore He says: 'God resists the proud, but gives grace to the

---

4. Jacob Preus, *Luther's Works, Volume 25 (Lectures on Romans)* (St. Louis, MO: Concordia Publishing House, 1972), 260.

humble. . . . Humble yourselves in the sight of the Lord, and He will lift you up" (James 4:6, 10, NKJV).

The problem of inflated self-image saturates our culture. When the College Board, a higher-education not-for-profit organization, asked high school seniors to compare themselves with their peers, zero percent viewed themselves as below average. Sixty percent ranked themselves in the top ten percent in "ability to get along with others." Social psychologists David Myers and Malcolm Jeeves conclude that "the most common error in people's self-image is not unrealistic low self-esteem, but rather self-serving pride; not an inferiority complex, but a superiority complex."[5]

The impact of Jesus's parable on the original audience would have been dramatic. The Pharisees would have rejected such a story; the crowd of onlookers would have been amazed; but the tax collectors, thieves, and others with a keen sense of their own spiritual need may have wept as Jesus declared the good news: it was possible for them to be forgiven and be justified before God.

Jesus ends the story with a sharp warning: "all those who exalt themselves will be humbled, and those who humble themselves will be exalted" (Luke 18:14).

5. David G. Myers and Malcolm A. Jeeves, *Psychology Through the Eyes of Faith* (San Francisco: HarperCollins, 1987), 209.

# 17

# THE PARABLE OF THE TWO SONS

Matthew 21:28–32

## The Story

"What do you think? There was a man who had two sons. He went to the first and said, 'Son, go and work today in the vineyard.'

"'I will not,' he answered, but later he changed his mind and went.

"Then the father went to the other son and said the same thing. He answered, 'I will, sir,' but he did not go.

"Which of the two did what his father wanted?"

"The first," they answered.

Jesus said to them, "Truly I tell you, the tax collectors and the prostitutes are entering the kingdom of God ahead of you. For John came to you to show you the way of righteousness, and you did not believe him, but the tax collectors and the prostitutes did. And even after you saw this, you did not repent and believe him."

—Matthew 21:28–32

## The Window

On the occasion that prompted this parable, Jesus entered the temple courts and was challenged by the chief priests and elders there:

Jesus entered the temple courts, and, while he was teaching, the chief priests and the elders of the people came to him. "By what authority are you doing these things?" they asked. "And who gave you this authority?"

Jesus replied, "I will also ask you one question. If you answer me, I will tell you by what authority I am doing these things. John's baptism—where did it come from? Was it from heaven, or of human origin?"

They discussed it among themselves and said, "If we say, 'From heaven,' he will ask, 'Then why didn't you believe him?' But if we say, 'Of human origin'—we are afraid of the people, for they all hold that John was a prophet."

So they answered Jesus, "We don't know."

Then he said, "Neither will I tell you by what authority I am doing these things" (Matthew 21:23–27).

After this exchange, Jesus tells the parable of the two sons. When the father asks his first son to work in the vineyard, the son initially answers with an abrupt, "I will not" (21:29). But later, he unexpectedly changes his mind and obeys his father's request.

When the father asks his second son the same question, this son gives what seems to be an admirable reply. The boy doesn't try to negotiate; he doesn't ask, "Do I have to go now? Must I stay all day? Which vineyard are you talking about? Will I get paid?" There is none of that. His response is clear, simple, and polite: "I will, sir" (v. 30).

Then the story takes a turn: The son who readily said yes to his father does not keep his word. Jesus offers no explanation for this son's behavior; he just does not go. He turns out to be "all hat and no cattle," as they say in Texas. His walk does not match his talk.

Jesus is clearly addressing the religious leaders of his day in this story. The Pharisees were good at knowing and interpreting the law. They professed a desire to please God and obey him—yet they did not receive Jesus's message of the kingdom. Nor did they listen when John the Baptist called them to repentance. They were outwardly compliant to the will of God, but inwardly resistant. This is why Jesus rebukes him: "For John came to you to show you the way of righteousness, and you did not believe him, but the tax collectors and the prostitutes did" (v. 32).

138

## The Mirror Shirley

Now, stepping back from this story for a moment, we must ask ourselves a question: "Where do I see myself in this story?"

Most people know something of the second son who says yes but doesn't follow through. In some ways, he's the father of everyone whose commitment goes no further than good intentions. At first glance, we might think that he is simply procrastinating; putting off the work; waiting for a more convenient time. We've all done that.

However, a closer look suggests that this son is more than just a procrastinator. Here is someone who wants to be identified with the father, but is not prepared to do the father's will. He wants the privileges of the kingdom, but not the responsibilities. He is willing to be a son—as long as there are no demands placed upon him.

On the other hand the first son, who initially says no but later obeys, provides hope for any and all who find themselves alienated from God. His story represents the gospel in a single sentence: "later he changed his mind and went" (v. 29). Here we have a portrait of the possibility of moving from no to yes.

As interesting as this story is, there seems to be an important detail missing: The story doesn't explain how or why the son who says no ends up saying yes. Why did he change his mind and finally do what his father asked? An equally important question is, why does the son who says yes end up not going?

The story tells us what happened, but we are left to wrestle with the "why" and "how." What keeps somebody with good intentions from following through? What empowers a no to become a yes?

This is important, because the journey from no to yes is *our* journey. We are all born with an innate no—Scripture describes it as our sinful nature. It is a "my will be done" rather than "thy will be done" attitude.

The kingdom of God, however, calls us to be willing to change—or, more accurately, *be* changed. God calls us to let go of our no and receive his yes. The kingdom of heaven is for those who hear the gospel, recognize their shortcomings, and accept their place in the kingdom.

Therefore, the story of the first son is not so much about obedience or even consistency as it is about the miracle of changing one's mind, heart, and will. This story highlights the grace of God that enables us to do the same.

Jesus doesn't spend any time exploring or explaining the motivations, characteristics, or circumstances that gave rise to the sons' behavior.

Perhaps that is because the story is not really about the two sons—it is, but it isn't. Jesus comes to the point of the parable when he says, "Truly I tell you, the tax collectors and the prostitutes are entering the kingdom of God ahead of you. For John came to you to show you the way of righteousness, and you did not believe him, but the tax collectors and the prostitutes did. And even after you saw this, you did not repent and believe him" (vv. 31–32).

Jesus told this parable to illustrate how the non-religious people of his day, the tax collectors and prostitutes, initially rejected God. Like the first son, they said no—but later experienced a change of heart and entered the kingdom. The second son represents the Jewish religious leaders of the day, who at first seemed to say yes to God, but ended up rejecting the kingdom. The parable calls us to consider the contrast between profession and practice—as Jesus asked, "Which of the two did what his father wanted?" (v. 31). This parable shows us that some people declare loyalty, compliance, and obedience yet never follow through.

The following story originally appeared in the British newspaper *The Guardian:*

A 69-year-old man was fined this week after officials discovered he hadn't shown up to work for at least six years. Ironically, the civil servant was discovered only when the deputy mayor attempted to give him an award for 20 years of "loyal and dedicated" service. "I thought, where is this man?" asked the deputy mayor. "Is he still there? Has he retired? Has he died?"

According to an internal report, a legal investigation was launched, which determined that the fellow hadn't been to his office for at least six years—and possibly much longer. He was supposed to be supervising the construction and maintenance of a water treatment plant. But the water company thought the man worked for the city (which he did) while the city council thought the water company was in charge of him. Another manager admitted to not having seen the man for years despite having an office directly across from his.

Once the missing man was finally located he said that he was given a job with no actual work to do so he just quit showing up.[1]

1. Michael Harthorne, "Man Skips Work for 6 Years; No One Notices," *USA Today,* February 15, 2016, https://www.usatoday.com/story/news/world/2016/02/14/man-skips-work-for-six-years/80378690/.

The man in the story said he would do his job, but he didn't. He gladly took his paycheck, but never did the work. This may be a point of particular application for those of us who are raised in Christian homes, attend Christian schools and/or colleges, or work in Christian organizations. Being part of Christian culture often leads others to assume that we follow God. But when we say yes, do we do so with a personal commitment to follow through?

It's easy to outwardly conform to Christian culture's expectations without making an inner commitment to follow Christ. In many settings, it's easy to project a Christian identity, proclaim a commitment to Christ, but privately live a life of disobedience. That is very dangerous.

In Matthew 7:21, Jesus says, "Not everyone who says to me, 'Lord, Lord,' will enter the kingdom of heaven, but only the one who does the will of my Father who is in heaven." Is there any chance that warning describes you? If, so, the parable has a further word.

The call to true discipleship demands that we follow through on our commitments to God. Discipleship is revealed not in what we say, but what we do. Jesus tells his disciples, "You are my friends if you do what I command" (John 15:14).

There was a young boy who used to sneak out of his house by crawling out of his bedroom window and onto the branches of an old fruit tree that stood by the house. Once he was in the tree, he would scamper to the ground and take off without his parents ever knowing he was gone.

One day, his father announced that he was thinking of chopping down the fruit tree since it hadn't borne any fruit for years. Later that day, fearing that he would lose his escape route, the boy bought a bushel of apples, and during the night, he tied the apples onto the barren branches.

The next morning, the man could not believe his eyes. He said to his wife, "Honey, I can't believe it! That old tree hasn't yielded any fruit for years, and now it's covered with apples. And the most amazing thing is—it's a pear tree!"

A few years ago, the editors of our university's magazine chose a Latin phrase as the theme of one of its issues: *esse quam videri*. It means, "To be, rather than to seem." This idea is at the heart of Jesus's parable.

The broader culture around us tends to invert this idea of *esse quam videri*. On one episode of his news satire show, *The Colbert Report*, Stephen Colbert sat in front of a fireplace that bore the inscription *videri quam esse*: "to seem, rather than to be." The phrase captured the whole premise of the show: Colbert seemed to be a serious reporter, but in reality, he wasn't. On television, it can humorous; in real life, it can be tragic.

Although this parable is relatively short and its message is direct, the lesson it teaches is profound. Salvation is not found in religion, keeping the law, or outwardly conforming to its practices—it is found in a relationship of love and service to God through Jesus Christ.

## Conclusion *Pastor*

The question is this: Where are you in this story that Jesus told? Have you said "no" to God, but now realize that you ought to say "yes"? Or perhaps you have said "yes," but never really followed through? This is a very serious issue. I think people are particularly vulnerable in that middle ground represented by the second son—acting like a Christian without really being a Christian. It's a perilous way to live.

The Bible says, "Be alert and of sober mind. Your enemy the devil prowls around like a roaring lion looking for someone to devour" (1 Peter 5:8). We have an enemy—Satan wants to rob God's people of every good thing in life. He will destroy your health; ruin your reputation; poison your relationships; break the hearts of those who love you; rob you of your plans and dreams for the future.

The Bible is clear when it says, "For the wages of sin is death." But there is good news—the verse that begins with, "For the wages of sin is death" ends with, "but the gift of God is eternal life in Christ Jesus our Lord" (Romans 6:23).

This is the clear witness of Scripture and the message of Jesus Christ: By his grace, we can be changed. We can start out saying no, but end up saying yes.

# 18

# THE PARABLE OF THE WEEDS

### The Story

Jesus told them another parable: "The kingdom of heaven is like a man who sowed good seed in his field. But while everyone was sleeping, his enemy came and sowed weeds among the wheat, and went away. When the wheat sprouted and formed heads, then the weeds also appeared.

"The owner's servants came to him and said, 'Sir, didn't you sow good seed in your field? Where then did the weeds come from?'

"'An enemy did this,' he replied.

"The servants asked him, 'Do you want us to go and pull them up?'

"'No,' he answered, 'because while you are pulling the weeds, you may uproot the wheat with them. Let both grow together until the harvest. At that time I will tell the harvesters: First collect the weeds and tie them in bundles to be burned; then gather the wheat and bring it into my barn.'"

—Matthew 13:24–30

Then [Jesus] left the crowd and went into the house. His disciples came to him and said, "Explain to us the parable of the weeds in the field."

He answered, "The one who sowed the good seed is the Son of Man. The field is the world, and the good seed stands for the people of the kingdom. The weeds are the people of the evil one, and the enemy

143

who sows them is the devil. The harvest is the end of the age, and the harvesters are angels.

"As the weeds are pulled up and burned in the fire, so it will be at the end of the age. The Son of Man will send out his angels, and they will weed out of his kingdom everything that causes sin and all who do evil. They will throw them into the blazing furnace, where there will be weeping and gnashing of teeth. Then the righteous will shine like the sun in the kingdom of their Father. Whoever has ears, let them hear."

—Matthew 13:36–43

## The Window

This story is unique to the Gospel of Matthew, who, fortunately, is also careful to include the interpretation Jesus gave his disciples after the crowd departed. As in many of Jesus's parables, the situation described came straight from his audience's everyday experiences. Farmers in Israel often had to contend with weeds that took root amid their crops.

The parable unfolds through a description of two sowers, two seeds, two responses, and final judgment followed by a solemn warning.

### Two Sowers

In the parable, there is a man who sows good seed in his field. While his workers are sleeping, the man's enemy comes and sows weeds among the wheat. In verses 37 and 39, Jesus identifies the two sowers: the one who sows the good seed is the Son of Man, the Lord Jesus; the one who sows the weeds is the devil.

This parable shows that Jesus Christ's kingdom does not go unopposed. The apostle Paul writes of this matter using the language not of agriculture, but of warfare: "For our struggle is not against flesh and blood, but against the rulers, against the authorities, against the powers of this dark world and against the spiritual forces of evil in the heavenly realms" (Ephesians 6:12). The Christian life is lived in a war zone, and if you are a believer in Jesus, you are in the trenches—there is real spiritual conflict.

Satan's ultimate goal is to rob Jesus of his glory. He wants people to look at the seeds Jesus sows—his church planted in the world—and find only weeds among them. He wants the world to notice the weeds more than the wheat—to see the hypocrites and frauds and those who say one thing on Sunday and another thing on Monday, and then suggest that Christians are no different from anyone else.

However, notice that even though Satan tries to sabotage the harvest, it is still the Son of Man who sows the good seed—who plants Christians in the world. The title "Son of Man" comes from the prophecy recorded in Daniel 7:13–14, where Daniel sees "one like a son of man" coming to "the Ancient of Days." And from the Ancient of Days—God the Father—the Son of Man receives dominion, authority, and a kingdom that shall never be destroyed.

It is this sovereign, mighty, conquering Son of Man, Jesus says, who, in the face of the enemy's malicious attempts to undermine God's sovereignty and defame God's name and glory, nevertheless plants his church in the world—and it does bear fruit in the end.

In explaining this parable, Christ declares that he is the sower. He spreads his redeemed seed, true believers, in the field of the world. When Jesus said, "The kingdom of heaven is at hand" (Matthew 3:2, 4:17, ESV), he was referring to the spiritual realm that exists on earth side-by-side with the realm of the evil one (1 John 5:19). When the kingdom of heaven comes in its fullness, heaven will be a reality, and there will be no weeds among the wheat. For now, however, both good and bad seeds mature in the world.

### Two Seeds

In the parable, the seeds the enemy sows are those of a poisonous weed known today as darnel. In the early stages of its growth, darnel closely resembles wheat. It is difficult, almost impossible, to distinguish wheat from darnel until both have matured and it is time for the harvest. Then the poisonous darnel has to be laboriously separated from the wheat:

> For many centuries, perhaps for as long as humans have cultivated cereal grains, wheat's evil twin has insinuated itself into our crops. In a big enough dose, this grass, darnel, can kill a person, and farmers would have to take care to separate it out from their true harvest—unless they were planning to add darnel to beer or bread on purpose, in order to get high.
>
> Darnel occupies a grey area in human agricultural history. It's definitely not good for us. When people eat its seeds, they get dizzy, off-balance and nauseous, and its official name, "temulentum," comes from a Latin word for "drunk."
>
> Darnel is a "mimic weed," neither entirely tame or quite wild, that looks and behaves so much like wheat that it can't live without human

assistance. Darnel seeds are stowaways: the plant's survival strategy requires its seeds to be harvested along with those of domesticated grasses, stored and replanted next season.[1]

## Two Responses

Once he finds that the field is contaminated, the farmer is faced with a dilemma: What should he do? The servants in verse 28 demonstrate one way to respond. Notice how zealous they are to take action when they find the weeds growing among the wheat: "Do you want us to go and pull them up?" They are quick to volunteer when they realize what the enemy has done. They are zealous about making things right—but their zeal is not in line with wisdom. They are being hasty, and the master of the field checks them.

"No," he says, "lest in gathering the weeds you root up the wheat along with them. Let both grow together until the harvest" (Matthew 13:29–30, ESV). In the visible church, among the good seed, there are always weeds to be found. The problem is that the sower's servants can't always distinguish between the two. Only the Son of Man can see the heart—thus, it's not our place to determine whether someone is saved or not. Only Jesus can safely make that determination, and when we try, more often than not, we do damage to the wheat while trying to remove the weeds.

The servants' desire to pull up the weeds that do not belong is a significant part of the story's tension. While their intentions are commendable, the landowner knows that such actions would do more harm than good. They must wait until the harvest.

## Final Judgment

At harvest time, the wheat and the darnel would be cut and taken to the threshing floor where the grain would be separated from the stalks. The wheat would be plump and golden-brown; darnel would be small and black. The servants would painstakingly separate one from the other, grain by grain, throwing out the darnel and keeping the wheat.

More than once, Jesus told his followers of an impending day of judgment. He warned them to watch out for false prophets in the meantime.

---

1. Sarah Laskow, "Wheat's Evil Twin Has Been Intoxicating Humans for Centuries," *Atlas Obscura*, last modified March 22, 2016, https://www.atlasobscura.com/articles/wheats-evil-twin-has-been-intoxicating-humans-for-centuries.

He said, "Beware of false prophets, who come to you in sheep's clothing, but inwardly are ravenous wolves" (Matthew 7:15, ESV).

## A Solemn Warning

As Jesus concludes his explanation of the parable, he offers a warning:

> As the weeds are pulled up and burned in the fire, so it will be at the end of the age. The Son of Man will send out his angels, and they will weed out of his kingdom everything that causes sin and all who do evil. They will throw them into the blazing furnace, where there will be weeping and gnashing of teeth. Then the righteous will shine like the sun in the kingdom of their Father. Whoever has ears, let them hear.
>
> (Matthew 13:40–43)

## The Mirror

The main point of application here is a warning against trying to separate the wheat from the weeds in our own power. Just as the owner of the field prohibited his servants from pulling up the weeds, it is not our role to judge other people—that is God's privilege alone. Just as the harvesters separate the weeds from the wheat at the end of the story, God will determine who is truly good and who is truly evil at the final judgment.

Unfortunately, there have been many times when well-meaning Christians, in an effort to purify the church, have caused irreversible damage. We know better than to stand in judgment of others—yet we do it anyway, particularly when it comes to the church. There is something deep inside us that wants to separate the sheep from the goats, the saints from the sinners, the good guys from the bad guys.

However, one has only to look at the Spanish Inquisition, the Crusades, and the reign of "Bloody Mary" to see the consequences of humanity's efforts to separate true believers from false. This is a task reserved for God alone. Even evil people have an opportunity to repent until the time of death. Instead of commanding for false believers to be rooted out of the world, possibly at the risk of hurting immature believers, Christ allows these people to remain until his return. At that time, angels will separate the true from the false believers. This is why the parable cautions us against premature judgment or criticism.

In his book, *Going Home*, Robert Raines describes what he pictures to be the church. He says, "It is not a neat, tidy sober congregation seated side by side in back-to-back pews facing forward, but a milling crowd, pushing, shoving, loving, laughing—a Moses-mob in the wilderness on its way to the Promised Land. It's not the righteous, but sinners, whom Jesus came to call."[2]

One additional thought for consideration is that, within any of us, there is the possibility of both wheat and weeds. Scripture speaks of a carnal nature that can remain within the heart of a believer, even after conversion. Mr. Rogers used to say: "Have you ever noticed that the very same people who are good sometimes are the very same people who are bad sometimes?"[3]

This brings to mind the familiar story called "Two Wolves." It goes like this: An old Cherokee man once told his grandson about a fight that was going on inside him. He said it was between two wolves. One was evil: anger, envy, greed, arrogance, self-pity, gossip, resentment, and false pride. The other was good: joy, peace, love, hope, serenity, humility, kindness, generosity, truth, compassion, and faith.

The grandson asked his grandfather, "Which wolf do you think will win?"

The old man replied, "The one I feed."

Scripture reminds us that we are born of the flesh and of the Spirit; we were created in the image of God, yet we bear the mark of original sin. As such, there resides within each of us the capacity for evil and the potential for good. The apostle Paul said of himself, "I do not understand what I do. For what I want to do I do not do, but what I hate I do" (Romans 7:15).

That is the second lesson of the parable, and the third is this: Ultimately, there will come a day of judgment. In the words of the parable, "Let both grow together until the harvest. At that time I will tell the harvesters: First collect the weeds and tie them in bundles to be burned; then gather the wheat and bring it into my barn" (Matthew 13:30).

### Conclusion

The good news of the parable is this: There is a harvest at the end. Despite Satan's best attempts to ruin it, the harvest comes. In other

2. Robert Raines, *Going Home* (New York: Crossroad Publishers, 1985), 118.

3. Fred Rogers, "Sometimes People are Good (1974)," *Mister Rogers' Neighborhood,* accessed September 2, 2019, https://www.misterrogers.org/video-playlist/mister-rogers-songs/.

words, the church is not destroyed; the church prospers. Satan's malice cannot derail the Son of Man's design for the salvation of sinners. What good news that is! It assures us that our confidence, our hope, and our future rest on him.

# AFTERWORD

They were amazed at his teaching, because his words had authority.

—Luke 4:32

The parables of Jesus are wonderful, but they were and are more than just stories. They open new windows into the kingdom and the heart of God. They provide a set of mirrors in which people—common folks as well as the scribes and Pharisees—can see themselves in the new light of the unfolding kingdom. In the parables, we meet ourselves and we meet God.

Jesus's stories were simple and memorable—yet he spoke with authority. Those who first heard the parables while seated at his feet were astonished at his teachings. His words brought understanding and encouragement. They were loaded with truth, but also with life—real, everyday life. His profound descriptions of life in the kingdom were tempered with a common touch that made his teachings authentic and accessible. And those stories are just as relevant to us today as they were when he first spoke them—they are hope-filled stories that help shift our focus toward eternity. While the world seeks to drown us in information, our souls thirst for wisdom. In the parables, we see life as we should—for in them, we see our gracious, patient, searching, and joyful God.

Near the end of her fine book titled *Surprised by Oxford: A Memoir*, Carolyn Weber reflects on her own unlikely conversion. As she looks back, she also looks forward, saying of her family, "I delight in children of our own and the promise of their discovering this God who loves them, too, in their own surprising ways. We will tell them our story and the story of how God loves a good story. And how he has authored a good story for each of us—the best story there was, and is, and ever will be."[1]

Her observations remind us that everyone loves a story—even God. He is the author of the greatest story ever told—the story of grace and redemption for all who will receive it through faith.

1. Carolyn Weber, *Surprised by Oxford: A Memoir* (Nashville: Thomas Nelson, 2011), 438.

# APPENDIX

The Parables of Jesus

1. The speck and the log (Matthew 7:1–6; Luke 6:37–42)
2. The two houses (Matthew 7:24–27; Luke 6:47–49)
3. Children in the marketplace (Matthew 11:16–19; Luke 7:31–35)
4. The two debtors (Luke 7:41–43)
5. The unclean spirit (Matthew 12:43–45; Luke 11:24–26)
6. The rich man's meditation (Luke 12:16–21)
7. The barren fig tree (Luke 13:6–9)
8. The sower (Matthew 13:3–9; Mark 4:3–20; Luke 8:5–8)
9. The weeds (Matthew 13:24–30)
10. The grain of mustard seed (Matthew 13:31–32; Mark 4:30–32; Luke 13:18–19)
11. The yeast (Matthew 13:33; Luke 13:20–21)
12. The lamp (Matthew 5:14–16; Mark 4:21–23; Luke 8:16–18; 11:33–36)
13. The dragnet (Matthew 13:47–52)
14. The hidden treasure (Matthew 13:44)
15. The pearl of great value (Matthew 13:45–46)
16. The householder (Matthew 13:52)
17. The marriage (Matthew 9:15; Mark 2:19–20; Luke 5:34–35)

18. The patched garment (Matthew 9:16; Mark 2:21; Luke 5:36)
19. The wine bottles (Matthew 9:17; Mark 2:22; Luke 5:37–39)
20. The harvest (Matthew 9:35–38; Luke 10:1–3)
21. Two insolvent debtors (Matthew 18:21–35)
22. The good Samaritan (Luke 10:25–37)
23. The three loaves (Luke 11:5–8)
24. The good shepherd (John 10:1–16)
25. The narrow gate (Matthew 7:13–14; Luke 13:22–30)
26. The guests (Luke 14:7–11)
27. The great banquet (Matthew 22:1–14; Luke 14:15–24)
28. The wedding clothes (Matthew 22:1–14)
29. The tower (Luke 14:28–30)
30. The king going to war (Luke 14:31–33)
31. The lost sheep (Matthew 18:10–14; Luke 15:4–7)
32. The lost coin (Luke 15:8–10)
33. The prodigal son (Luke 15:11–32)
34. The unjust steward (Luke 16:1–15)
35. The rich man and Lazarus (Luke 16:19–31)
36. The slave's duty (Luke 17:7–10)
37. Laborers in the vineyard (Matthew 20:1–16)
38. The talents (Matthew 25:14–30; Luke 19:11–27)
39. The importunate widow (Luke 18:1–8)
40. The Pharisee and tax-gatherer (Luke 18:9–14)
41. The two sons (Matthew 21:28–32)
42. The wicked vine-growers (Matthew 21:33–44; Mark 12:1–11; Luke 20:9–18)
43. The fig tree (Matthew 24:32–35; Mark 13:28–31; Luke 21:29–33)
44. The watching servant (Matthew 24:42–44; Luke 12:35–40)
45. The man on a journey (Mark 13:32–34)
46. Character of two servants (Matthew 24:45–51; Luke 12:42–46)
47. The ten virgins (Matthew 25:1–13)
48. The vine and branches (John 15:1–17)